Advance Praise for Group Alchemy

You, too, can realize a 100 percent increase in productivity.

Group Alchemy is a unique and powerful book about groups and teams. It provides some of the best advice available about how to master the elements of a framework for collaboration—one that I know works—and weave your own fabric of success. And it completely honors the human spirit (no "tips and tricks for better manipulating your pesky teammates"), so you can absorb and apply its teachings with integrity.

What I love about *Group Alchemy* is the reader's opportunity to take any of its many, many exquisitely and artfully offered gems about how to work better with others and apply them today. Then repeat! This is the essence of mastery.

Go ahead: dare to go your own way. Dare to do what works. Read and apply *Group Alchemy*. You, too, can realize a 100 percent increase in productivity and have much more satisfaction at work.

—Christopher Avery PhD, founder of the growing worldwide Leadership Gift movement and author of *Teamwork Is an Individual Skill.*

The book I wish I'd had when I was setting up a new organization!

Often when we work with stellar consultants, we wish they'd give us a "how to" manual. And here it is! *Group Alchemy* is a step-by-step, values-driven guide to organizational change written by someone with intellectual power *and* years of field experience. This is the book I wish I'd had when I was setting up a new organization! I look forward to using it with staff, volunteers, and board development groups.

—Anne Jennings, nonprofit founder, director, board member

I am delighted to have these fresh, powerful tools to move my work forward.

In each of the six major sections of *Group Alchemy*, I was struck repeatedly by Dr. Pruitt's deep insight into the roots of the human foibles that have so often derailed success in the groups I've worked with. More practically, I was quite taken with the logic and clarity of the solutions she offers for getting past roadblocks or avoiding them in the first place. I am delighted to have these fresh, powerful tools to move my work forward.

—John B Dahl, senior fellow, director, education, THX Ltd.

You'll want to keep this treasure close at hand and refer to it often!

Useful for everyone who works with others to get things done, this book is brimming with practical guidance on how to cultivate a group culture that supports masterful collaboration and gets results. In *Group Alchemy* we benefit from all the wisdom Deborah's gained during nearly three decades of research and experience working with groups, distilled into the six elements that are essential to group success. All the while she holds for us a vision of what is possible when we adopt the practices of masterful collaboration. You'll want to keep this treasure close at hand and refer to it often!

—Sharon Coviak, CPA, manager of securities analysis, Fannie Mae

Group Alchemy can work for high-functioning teams looking for their next mountain to climb as well as groups stuck in politics, dissention, and weak results.

Deborah Pruitt brings an anthropologist's eye, twenty-five years of experience advising groups, and passionate creativity to unlocking the secrets of group success. *Group Alchemy* is a powerful new touchstone for anyone interested in transformational performance in a group setting. It can work for high-functioning teams looking for their next mountain to climb as well as groups stuck in politics, dissention, and weak results. The six building blocks or principles of group alchemy are easy to follow and practical for those facing real-world challenges. Deborah Pruitt is a "Passion Capitalist" who offers valuable and original insights to leaders. Read the book and experience the true magic of *Group Alchemy*.

—Paul Alofs, author, *Passion Capital—The World's Most Valuable Asset*

Group Alchemy

*The Six Elements
of Highly Successful
Collaboration*

Deborah Pruitt

For the gold within your group

Printed in the United States of America.
Book design by Meadowlark Publishing Services.
Cover illustration by Barbara Lande, Lande Designs.

ISBN 978-0-9857532-0-7

Published 2012.

Published by Group Alchemy Publishing.
www.groupalchemy.net
Group Alchemy® is a registered trademark.

al • che • my [al-kem-mee]
noun

1. a medieval chemical science and speculative philosophy aiming to achieve the transmutation of base metals into gold
2. a power or process of transforming something common into something special

group • al • che • my [groop al-kem-mee]
noun

1. a process of transforming individuals into a powerful group that creates excellent results and positive experiences for its members
2. the optimized performance of a group of people
3. a state of being a powerful group

To Larry, my favorite alchemist—
without whom this book would not exist.

And to all those who seek to make the world a better place.

Contents

Preface

This book began almost thirty years ago—though I didn't know it then.

I was working for a cutting-edge consumer electronics start-up as its national sales coordinator. It was an exciting opportunity and we were getting a lot of recognition for the innovative products we offered.

But over time my initial enthusiasm for the company was dashed. Internal politics and poor management created many obstacles to the success we had originally imagined for the company. I felt repeatedly blocked by internal politics from contributing my best work to our mission of delivering outstanding audio and video products. I left the company frustrated and disappointed that my talents and abilities had been so frequently wasted.

This experience was key to my subsequent life's work. I was baffled. How could a company so committed to becoming a global leader in technology (one that had the premier video product of its time, no less) be so ineffective at utilizing the talent it had acquired?

A Pivot in a New Direction: Anthropology

I could easily have left that job in search of greener pastures with another company. But this wasn't the first time I'd been disappointed participating in groups in the workplace. My cumulative experiences with a variety of companies had brought me to a threshold; my intellectual curiosity was piqued. What *was* it about organizations that set up barriers to the full expression of the talents and creativity of their members? I decided to go back to school to search for an explanation.

This wasn't going to be as simple as taking a few business courses about motivating people to excel or effective conflict resolution, though there were plenty of those around. I had bigger questions about the nature of human behavior that could only be explored by studying anthropology. If I wanted to understand people well enough to comprehend the problematic patterns I'd found in groups, I reasoned, it made sense to learn from people all over the world. I embarked on a remarkable journey, one that led me to see the world through many different cultural viewpoints. When I secured a National Science

Foundation Fellowship for a PhD program at the University of California at Berkeley, I knew I had found my calling.

Once I took the plunge and entered the field of anthropology, I let my curiosity lead me. I roamed broadly through anthropological theory, linguistics, philosophy, and theories of social change while also studying organizational and management theory from an anthropological perspective. I gradually became interested in understanding all forms of organizing, especially alternatives to bureaucratic and hierarchical organizations. For two years I studied grassroots organizations in Jamaica while learning to enter deeply into another culture. This gave me a first-hand understanding of how culture shapes and constrains human behavior as well as how culture is produced and reproduced. I completed my dissertation on a topic that fascinated me: the impact of tourism on cultural identity and economic development.

My Work with Groups

After receiving my doctorate, I returned to my interest in work organizations and spent many years as a consultant to values-centered organizations. My aim was to help them become more effective, sharpen their focus of purpose, clarify their identity, and improve their ability to structure their work to achieve their goals.

At the same time, I taught classical anthropology, earning tenure at Laney College in Oakland. Working with students to help them understand the dynamics of culture, differences in cultural perspectives, and how to become conscious of their own cultural viewpoint taught me even more about how to see culture at work.

Over time the connections between my work as an anthropologist and my work as an organizational consultant—seemingly very disparate endeavors—became clear. This combination now forms the basis of my insights into what helps groups work and how to help people transform a haphazardly developed culture into one that supports their aspirations. I have come to the conclusions I present in this book by seeking answers to this question: *What are the essential attributes of powerfully successful groups?* I needed both disciplines to formulate the answers; what I came to call group alchemy can be thought of as the anthropology of groups. This is a holistic, cultural approach to building powerful leadership and collaboration in effective groups.

To uncover the attributes of successful groups, I had to witness and document, repeatedly, what outstanding groups actually *do* that works to connect people in common interests and collective actions. By combining those practices with a model of culture, I discovered that there is a predictable and reliable way to generate a creative alchemy in any group and sustain an environment in which everyone can excel. I also learned that producing results does not have to come at the expense of high-quality relationships and personal experiences. In fact, these have to occur together if successful results are to be sustained over time. This is that special chemistry that lights people up when they talk about the great results and working environments they enjoy.

In my consulting work I share my discoveries at the intersection of organization and culture. For the groups who delve into this system, the potential is enormous; I've witnessed its transformative impact. My quest has been to bring profound insights from scholarly research and organizational practice into a practical, culturally based method that empowers individuals and their groups to achieve their visions for the world. I am convinced that any group working with these concepts and practical suggestions can improve its effectiveness and enhance the lives of its members. My hope is that this book will make it easy for you to do that.

Acknowledgments

A life's work such as this involves far more people than I could possibly thank here. Yet I find I must try to acknowledge the people who have influenced me and contributed so much to my life and this work.

First I have to thank the people in Jamaica who accepted this stranger in their midst as a young graduate student and who taught me so much about life and culture. The generous people across all the countries I have visited and lived in have touched me deeply and taught me much about how to bridge differences and create collaboration.

Then there are the many clients and organizations that honored me by inviting me to help them further their missions. They in turn taught me so much; every one of those conversations and interactions is present here in some way because they are embedded in my perspective on what works to help people achieve their dreams.

I am indebted to my fellow scholars, colleagues and teachers—academic and spiritual—who have shaped me. The richness of their writings, ideas, and conversation is my context. And thanks to the students who are my teachers as well, reminding me of the value in giving up pretensions of "knowing it all" in favor of the power of collaboration in the pursuit of knowledge and wisdom.

There are crucial moments in any project when just the right input marks the difference between success and failure. That came to me in the form of a great editing team. It's impossible to express the gratitude I feel toward Sheridan McCarthy and Stan Nelson at Meadowlark Publishing Services for their terrific guidance and patient diligence. The quality of their editing is a revelation to me.

The encouragement and confidence I've received from those closest to me and my work are what made this book possible: BB Borowitz, Mary Gaetjens, Anne Jennings, Nicki Norman, Jenny Michael, John Dahl. Thanks to my friend Barbara Lande for finding such a beautiful way to graphically represent my vision.

Finally, there truly are no words to express the gratitude I have for my husband and partner, Larry Jenson. His faith in me, his commitment to our relationship, and our work together nourish all that I do.

Introduction

If you want to go fast, go alone.
If you want to go far, go together.
—African proverb

As this proverb suggests, when we want to go far and accomplish big things in the world, we need the power and resources of a group of people. But simply forming a group is no guarantee of success. We all know that some groups succeed while others fail. Some are a pleasure to work in while others are miserable. But why? What is the secret of a truly successful group, in which everyone is inspired and energized, creative thinking prevails, great accomplishments are routine, and people feel connected and fulfilled?

This book, a product of twenty-five years of study, answers these questions. Group success is not a mystery, a matter of chance, or dependent upon a charismatic leader. Rather, it is the result of building a conscious culture within the group. It is achieved through core practices I have seen work again and again and through which groups achieve things that seemed impossible before. An executive team negotiates its $300 million budget in two days instead of arguing for a month as it did the previous year. After a year of struggling, a board of directors finds desperately needed new members within a few weeks. Staff members resolve old tensions, begin speaking to each other again, and come to appreciate their different perspectives—and the entire group benefits from improved communication and the creative interplay of ideas. I have witnessed such transformations in my work many times, and many others like them.

I have crafted the practices that generate such positive results into a systematic and replicable method I call *the group alchemy formula*. If you fully engage your group in this system, you will ensure that it becomes capable of high-level performance and achieves ever-higher levels of effectiveness over time—regardless of what the world happens to throw your way.

When you are equipped with the ideas and tools this formula contains and have the determination to put them to use, there is nothing to stand between your group and the rapid and powerful improvements in effectiveness I have seen again and again in other groups through the years.

Is This Book for You?

I wrote this book for people who are committed to making a difference in the world and want a reliable way to consistently build the powerful relationships that can make that happen. It speaks to the formal leaders and managers of groups, and it speaks to inspired group members who want to work more effectively.

This book is for you if:

- Your business or cause is being asked to accomplish more with less and you need to know that you are tapping into the full potential of your combined talents.

- You want your workplace to be outstandingly productive and personally fulfilling but it has undercurrents of dissatisfaction or tension.

- You wish it were easier to reach decisions as a group. You're tired of meetings that are tedious and accomplish little.

- You would like to know skillful ways to prevent the problems that lead to unproductive conflict, distractions, petty grievances, and resentment.

- You wish your team had better communication, more creativity, and greater openness to new ideas.

- You want to eliminate the "drama" in your group and enjoy your work more.

Unless you have a clear and certain path for creating powerful collaboration—a method you can trust—you're at the mercy of individual personalities or the vagaries of group dynamics. When it's left to chance, achieving consistently successful collaboration seems mysterious. Even when the group comes together well, it can seem largely a matter of chance. If you don't solve the mystery of group success, it can be difficult to sustain or so personality based that it's vulnerable to even the smallest change in personnel.

The Need for a New Way

My training as a cultural anthropologist and my many years of facilitating group development in a wide variety of organizations have shown me that most groups never realize the tremendous potential of the wealth of talent and expertise they possess. I think this is because so many of the methods we draw upon for structuring and running our organizations are based on conventional management concepts that actually limit what a group can accomplish. The command-and-control ideology at the core of most management theories often leaves people who are not at the top echelons of the company feeling alienated, distrusted, and disrespected. This is the product of such practices as holding key information secret, setting arbitrary rules, and failing to involve people in decisions that affect them. Even when enlightened managers in conventional companies do their best to lead their small groups respectfully, the context of command-and-control rather than collaboration leaves much creativity and productivity by the wayside.

This is not news. Throughout the last century there has been a steady trend in management theory (and some practice) away from highly authoritarian and bureaucratic management toward more participatory ways of managing. This is known to be especially important in groups of educated professionals who value self-determination and have many choices about where they work. I think it's important everywhere.

Simply put, the old top-down management ideas are not satisfactory or sufficient. We need more potent methods for negotiating the social environment of working together, particularly in the face of significant differences in social and cultural backgrounds, generations, personalities, and experience. Groups like many of those I have consulted with, such as nonprofit organizations, boards of directors, professional partnerships, coalitions, associations of member organizations, and small businesses, need alternatives to directing and controlling. We need more honorable ways to draw from the talent, wisdom, creativity, and insight in our groups so we can solve the very complex problems facing us.

When I began to work with groups struggling to develop effective collaboration, I found there was no comprehensive, holistic model sufficient to serve as a guide for practical development. The lack of such a model is, I believe, the source of uncertainty and reticence about collaboration. It is the reason for the fear that anything less than tight control will lead to inefficiency or even chaos. In reality, strong collaboration has the opposite effect—much greater efficiency and far less confusion. Attention to the inner workings of your group isn't incidental, a luxury, or "touchy-feely" stuff that distracts from your "real" work: it's an essential part of your work if you are genuinely pursuing excellence. And this book contains the missing model for doing this work.

Building a Culture of Collaboration

Culture is the key to successful groups because it's the frame of reference that defines what people believe is possible and which actions they choose to take. This makes it the driver of events. *Every* group of people that interacts routinely develops a culture, whether it forms one consciously or not. The task before you is to make sure that your culture supports your mission. You can do this by consciously creating a unique culture attuned to your particular group's identity, values, and ambitions—one that calls for the behaviors that satisfy those ambitions.

A culture is created and reproduced by all the members of the group, brick by brick, through daily practices—the sometimes large but often small behaviors and customs people engage in as a matter of course. It's not something that can be designed, changed, or implemented from the top down. That is a fundamental misunderstanding of how culture actually works, and it stems from a bias toward control. Such attempts are really nothing more than a new management strategy, one that adopts the word "culture."

The fact is that *culture is co-created*—always. It is in the mundane, day-to-day interactions of people at every level of an organization that values, beliefs, and commitments are either kept or broken. It is in these interactions that behaviors that express and support the values and results to which the group is committed must be established and nourished. It begins in face-to-face workgroups and scales from there.

What individuals do is critical to group success. But the highest level of success available depends on *what groups do together:* the shared practices that build a culture to connect people in common interests and actions. As the group works together to replace unconscious, unproductive habits with conscious, effective ones, the culture that emerges transcends any particular individual and is not dependent upon who is in the group. Such an inspired culture becomes the context for everything you do and gives rise to the behavior that creates the success you seek. The higher the degree of conscious practice, the greater the group's capacity to develop its wealth of talents and expertise and achieve ever higher levels of success.

The group alchemy formula guides you easily and incrementally through this conscious creation of culture.

The Group Alchemy Formula

As I connected my knowledge of how culture works with my efforts to create more effective organizations, I realized that there are six fundamental sets of practice that characterize and define highly functioning groups. I call these practices *elements* because they are the fundamental, irreducible aspects of culture that address the requirements all social groups face: inspiring and uniting their members; organizing and managing activities; and learning, adapting, and rejuvenating themselves. Each element is a necessary condition for a highly successful group, and it is their synthesis that generates full capability in groups. Together they make up the group alchemy formula.

The six elements of the formula are *inspiration, agreements, accountability, acknowledgment, renewal,* and *mastery.*

The names of these elements may seem familiar to you, but as I use them here there are significant distinctions that represent uncommon understandings of these words.

Each respective chapter explores these transformative dimensions so you can access their full potential.

I have written this book to be a practical guide based on the fundamental principle that positive transformation of a group occurs when unconscious beliefs, assumptions, and habits become conscious. To achieve this practical guidance, each chapter leads you systematically through one of the elements. You will assess how your group currently performs in each one, learn what works for you and what doesn't, develop new shared practices that work, and establish structures to sustain your effectiveness in each of these key areas.

When your group has carefully considered each element and made conscious choices about what you stand for and how you will work together, you have access to your group's full creative alchemy.

The Promise of Group Alchemy

Every group can increase its success by working in the elements described here. If you are struggling, you will find that applying this formula will get you unstuck and on the road to success. If your group is already working successfully, you can use this formula to take it to the next level and increase your impact. If you are forming a group, applying the formula guarantees that you will craft a powerful organization in which everyone takes responsibility for the success of the enterprise. And you will avoid the pitfalls that derail so many groups over time.

Whatever your situation, working in this formula will make it easier to attract people and resources that can contribute to your purpose. And it will make it easier to adapt and generate accomplishments while navigating a changing world.

You've worked hard to be great at what you do. Why not apply comparable effort toward being great at working together? A small initial investment of time to establish your core practices together will pay handsome dividends by reducing time spent unproductively in the future. Even small changes can have significant impact. The pages that follow are full of inspiring stories and examples of what you can do. The important thing is to begin.

Inspiring the Future

A vision of what we want to see in the world is what calls us forward and inspires us to take action. Such inspiration is the starting point for any accomplishment and all transformation. And so the formula begins in chapter 1 with the element of inspiration.

Element One:

Inspiration

Energize and unite your group

Clarify a common purpose

Realize excellence

Don't ask yourself what the world needs.
Ask yourself what makes you come alive, and then go do that.
Because what the world needs is people who have come alive.
— Dr. Howard Thurman

We begin our exploration of the elements of group alchemy with the answer to the fundamental and ongoing challenge that faces all groups—how to connect people's passions and individual interests so that they "come alive" *together* in shared resolve around a compelling vision for the future. A collection of people pursuing their own interests has limited potential while a group of people working together based on shared interests is capable of greatness. *How will people come to see their personal interests, their dreams and aspirations, as linked? What will connect people together powerfully enough that they will cast their lot with the group, commit to genuine collaboration, and work in concert?*

We all take action in the world to meet our needs and achieve our dreams. Because we cannot survive, let alone thrive, on our own, we join with others to pursue our ambitions. But since we no longer live in the traditional, homogeneous communities of our ancestors, we are generally joining groups that contain great diversity of backgrounds, personal styles, and motivations. The more congruent our diverse personal motivations are with the purpose of the groups we are in, the more successful we can all be. Such congruence is achieved through the conscious practice of inspiration.

This chapter describes the set of practices that persuade people to work together to achieve something that can only be accomplished by a group. We will review the components of powerful group inspiration, the mind-set and distinct qualities that make it a powerful catalyst for accomplishment, and the practices you can put in place to help the people in your group stay so inspired that you will excel in everything you do.

In the presence of profound inspiration, people's deepest motivations are ignited into powerful actions; they can see the opportunity to achieve their personal goals and the chance to be a part of something greater than themselves. In such an environment, remarkable things are possible. The process of alchemy—which I defined in the introduction as the transformation of something mundane into something extraordinary—has begun.

The inspiration task in group alchemy is to establish a compelling purpose and authentic identity and make them active forces throughout the organization.

Unifying Diversity

Until recently, our ancestors met their needs for survival and belonging in the family and community groups they were born into, but we live in different times. We join most of the groups we participate in today by choice. This means that most groups are made up of a diverse collection of people from different backgrounds and personal motivations. And that reality creates both opportunity and challenge: opportunity because we can draw from the strengths found in a wide variety of backgrounds and abilities, challenge because we don't have sufficient shared traditions to make it easy to come together. The puzzle we must solve is how to integrate diverse backgrounds and styles in collaboration. The solution begins with inspiration and runs all the way through the group alchemy formula.

Declaring Shared Inspiration

In the formula for group alchemy, the term *inspiration* refers to the set of declarations, statements, stories, conversations, and practices that articulate and animate the *vision, purpose, and identity* of the group.

This practice begins with answering the questions: *What future are we creating in the world? What is the purpose of this group? What kind of group will we be?* All groups answer these questions in some manner, declaring what I like to refer to as "who we are and what we're up to." Some groups do this more intentionally than others and enjoy greater success as a result.

Powerful groups answer these questions together in an explicit conversation about the impact they intend to create in the world. This conversation defines a shared future. It describes a distinctive identity for the group that encompasses how the group will collaborate to bring its vision and purpose to fruition. It is the *experience* of having this conversation that allows members to see how their personal interests and ambitions link with the group. This is where the alchemy of transforming a collection of individuals into a powerful group begins.

Defining Purpose Unites

Nuestra Casa is a nonprofit organization that serves a rural Latino immigrant community. When the board of directors asked me to help them with a strategic plan, I began by asking them about their mission. They showed me a mission statement that had been created several years earlier for a grant proposal by someone no longer in the organization. None of the current board or staff were involved in creating it. They said that the words did not resonate with them, so we set to work clarifying their vision and mission.

As I asked them what they cared enough about that they would give up a beautiful Saturday to volunteer their free time to the organization, we gradually uncovered the meaning the work held for them. Each member told a deeply personal story about the struggles they had overcome in their own lives and how they saw this organization as an opportunity to make it easier for others to avoid or overcome similar difficulties. As I recorded their words on flip charts and they discussed and debated their meanings and priorities, their collective inspiration began to emerge. The moment we identified the words that summed up what motivated them—what became their vision and mission statements—there was a palpable feeling in the room as everyone relaxed and smiled. "Yes, that's it!" they said. "*That* is what we are about."

Through this conversation, all of the individuals reconnected with what had inspired them to do this work in the first place. Since that time this group has drawn upon their clarity of inspiration to persevere through crippling cuts in state funding and difficult changes in staffing, and the group continues to serve the community while attracting new support.

What ultimately matters is that when we are inspired our deepest personal motivations can be turned into powerful actions. Consider the times you stood against the odds and created something that meant a great deal to you, or a time when you gave up a weekend for a project you were excited about or in order to meet an important deadline: this is what happens when people are focused on their inspiration.

When an entire group is inspired together, the extraordinary becomes possible. Inspired people become champions for the cause, dedicated to the success of the group enterprise. They refuse to let anything stand in their way and will make personal sacrifices in the interest of what they believe can be achieved. They are alert to opportunities and sensitive to dangers and risks. They are not complacent; they cannot overlook weaknesses or interference that might stand in the way of success.

The Power of Story

Because inspiration conversations tap participants' deep desires and sense of meaning, they generate narratives that shape perceptions, define what seems possible, and guide behavior. This is the first essential step in creating the culture that will shape *what people actually do*. It works because you are involved in a timeless cultural process that engages the *power of story*.

All cultures use story to explain the world, their place in it, and how to live a "good life." I call these *defining stories*. Such stories, passed down through the generations, have held cultures together for thousands of years. They are the way we organize information, and they are what holds any group together. They unite us in a *web of meaning* that everyone understands. They enable the group to coalesce, and they become its steadfast guides.

While I use the words "story" or "statement," which you might think of as static—

The Stories We Live By

The power of story that we are exploring here comes from the foundation of culture in *myth*. I know the word myth can have negative connotations, because the word is often used derogatorily as a way to dismiss something as untrue. But if we understand the profound significance myth has played in the human experience and how it shapes what people do, we can better understand the power of story in our groups today. The fact is that myth is operating in every group—whether or not it is understood as such.

Myths are the stories that people in all cultures have created and passed down through the generations to explain the world and their place in it. This is true whether the origin story is the Judeo-Christian story of Yahweh, the life of Buddha, or the Hopi Indian story of Spider Woman. As children grow up in the society, they learn who they are and how to act in concert with the group through these stories. In this way, myths are the foundations of culture.

The question of whether a people's stories are "true" according to someone else's standards is irrelevant to understanding them. They reflect truth as the people who hold and preserve the story see it. As their truth, the shared perspective that comes from these stories *connects people in a common identity, provides guidelines for their behavior, and inspires them to take appropriate action in the world*. These are powerful functions that account for their ability to confer a deep sense of belonging among community members. Stories continue to play an important role to this day and for the same reasons. *We are exquisitely adapted to understand our world and our place in it through stories.*

When you engage in intentional conversations to articulate your purpose and values, you create unifying narratives: myths, not unlike the ancient ones, that connect the members of the group in a shared identity that shapes behavior and guides the myriad choices they must make every day for the cause of "getting things done."

The inspiration element is about calling on this human heritage and working in the realm of myth in a conscious way that serves your larger purpose. When you keep the power of narrative alive and present in day-to-day moments through personal habits and group customs, you capture the full power of myth for your collective purposes.

written or spoken in a set way and then passed along—it is important to understand that in reality these are *active conversations* that involve everyone in the group intentionally choosing, engaging, and acting from a vision of what it is committed to. We will look into this further in the Principles of Practice Section. For now, let's look more closely at the kinds of stories that frame group inspiration.

Key Defining Stories That Frame Inspiration for Groups

The primary stories that connect people in shared purpose fall into three categories: the *vision* for the world that the group seeks to create, the *practical* approach the group will take to do so, and the *identity* the group wants or must have in order to accomplish its purpose. In formal organizations they have been given the names *vision statements, mission statements, and values statements.* I have added one to the group alchemy formula; I call it *identity statements.*

The first three names are probably familiar to you; for decades now organizations have been encouraged to create vision and mission statements, even if some do so only as offhand prerequisites to annual reports, business and strategic plans, or fundraising efforts. Sadly, this means that many organizations' vision and mission statements fail to deliver their full potential.

The forms these take are usually concise statements but may also include longer narratives. This is less important than the way they are created and how they are applied.

I describe each kind of statement briefly here; then throughout the chapter I will explore the particular qualities that distinguish powerful inspiration and how to work with it so you can benefit from the full potential of your defining stories.

Vision Stories of What We Stand For

I've come to the conclusion that the most important thing people want in a leader is someone who can articulate a vision that they get excited about.
—Mark Laret, CEO, UCSF Medical Center

These stories describe the desire to be part of something that connects us to the world beyond ourselves. Each of us may express that impulse differently, but always in terms of *value to others.*

Explicit Shared Stories Can Benefit Everyone
All groups that want to achieve something—businesses, volunteer groups, community action groups, or any collection of people who need to articulate a basis for coming together—will benefit from consciously creating their own stories.

Subgroups within organizations (departments, teams, task groups) need their own inspiration too, a story that links to the larger organizational mission and identity. Often, this is not well understood, and an opportunity to develop the capacity of smaller departments and work groups is missed.

Your marriage and your family will also be strengthened through clearly articulated inspiration stories that declare who you are and what you are committed to.

Vision—the Destination

The beginning of every great achievement is a vision of a possibility in the world that the group exists to create or advance. *What future world are we creating? When we have done our job, how will the world be improved or changed?*

Core Values—the Compass

The group's purpose is grounded in the values the members care most deeply about and that serve as guidelines for the group's actions and choices. *What do we stand for? What are we willing to work for and not compromise?*

Practical Stories About What We Do

The lofty realms of possibility and vision require practical plans for how to go about creating that inspiring world. This is the province of mission, strategic plans, and goals.

Mission—the Route

To create the world we said was worth working for in our vision, we must choose a course of action: a mission. The mission answers this question: *What will we do in order to achieve our vision?*

Goals and Strategies—the Milestones

Goals and strategies make the mission believable by describing specific results the group will accomplish along the way to achieving its mission. By being specific in terms of actions, outcomes, and a timeline, a group can assess its progress and make adjustments when needed to stay on target. *What specific milestones will help us to achieve our mission and assess our progress along the way?*

Identity Stories of Who We Are

Once you know what you're working for and how you will pursue it, you can answer the question, *Who do you have to be (as an individual, a group, and as an organization) in order to create that world?*

This conversation gets more specific about the climate and culture necessary for the group to be maximally productive *and* a positive place for its members. Too often this is the piece that is left out of organizational development. As we go through the group alchemy formula, you will see how important a statement of group identity is and the substantial value it can generate in your group's results.

Identity—the Vehicle

This story expresses the commitment you're making to the kind of group you will be: how members will treat each other, your customers, and your community in order to fulfill your mission. *How does our group need to look and act to support our success?*

History and Tradition Stories—the Journey

All groups have traditions and defining moments that have shaped who they are and what matters to them. Stories that capture the essence of who you aspire to be are valuable. *How were we created as an organization or group? What important transitions or critical times has our group survived that help to define us and show us what we are capable of?* Together these stories of vision, purpose, and identity form an overarching narrative for the group that defines what you will be responsible and accountable for because they articulate what you care most about and are committed to.

The key to the alchemy in these stories is that when they are shared—through conversations, stories, and written documents—you are able to create and re-create inspiration in the group. They are a wellspring of inspiration you can draw from again and again; each time you share them, you replenish the well as you catalyze the power of individual passion into collective action.

Perhaps you have already developed these conversations in your group. If you haven't, your first task is to start. If you are having them, then your task is to keep them percolating through your daily activities.

Wherever your group is in this process, the rest of this chapter will help you work powerfully together to remain engaged in an inspiring narrative. This will guide, direct, inspire, and energize everyone in the context of what you agree to be and do together.

Now let's look more closely at how intentional inspiration practices work to fuel the power of groups.

The Alchemy of Inspiration

Explicit, well-articulated stories about what is possible—inspiration stories—can lead to extraordinary results. Let's investigate some of their transformational effects.

People Achieve Excellence

Creating a big story of "what we're up to" gives meaning to small, day-to-day tasks by providing *context*. People work to their best ability and give their most when they know they fit into a framework that holds a vision of what their work means. Consider the following parable:

> A traveler came across a group of masons chipping stone. He asked one of the men, "What are you doing?" The mason answered, "I'm chipping stone." As the traveler walked farther he saw that one man's work looked far superior to the rest and that he appeared to be enjoying what he was doing. The traveler asked, "What are you doing?" The mason answered enthusiastically, "I'm building a cathedral!"

The inspired mason produced exceptional results because he held a clear vision of what his small piece of the effort would ultimately accomplish: a grand cathedral for the ages. This was his context and it transformed his work from an execution of tasks to the enactment of purpose. An inspiring context can transform anyone's task in the same way, whether they work in the boardroom or the maintenance yard.

People Focus

Possibilities and opportunities abound in this world, and they can lure your attention away from what you've already decided to commit to. Challenges and difficulties can distract you from what excites you about participating in a group. But clearly articulated inspiration stories keep the focus on what excites you no matter what else may ebb and flow around you. They keep you connected to the group, eager to do its work and keep its momentum going.

People Act in Concert

Defining stories provide clear parameters for choosing what actions to take, and this means that people can act within the same framework. Like band members unified by the same musical score, each member of the group performs a part in shaping the future, improvising where appropriate and adding their own special dimension to the emerging creation. The results are an integrated whole and unified motion.

People Take Initiative

Inspiration that is collectively created and validated empowers people throughout the organization to act responsibly and with great energy on behalf of the group's overall purpose and the specific outcomes it desires. When everyone knows their value in the group and how they are aligned with everyone else, they can be confident that their actions are "rational"—that they fit with the overarching goals. This kind of confidence inspires initiative and creativity that a lesser-inspired group would find unthinkable. Inspired people are alert to opportunities and sensitive to dangers and risks.

Collectivism Trumps Individualism

In an inspired group, the vision creates communal strength that expands the sense of self to include relationship with others, which forms the basis for generosity. Providing assistance to others in the group makes sense because "helping them helps me." Power struggles shrink as people identify with a common purpose and goals. They can let go of being right and getting credit and instead act for the sake of what works for the cause.

We often see this in organizations at their beginning, when there is a powerful idea that stimulates people to give it their all. The passion on which many startups are founded may inspire people to sleep at the office and work round the clock to ensure they make a full contribution to the whole. We also see it when organizations face such serious threats that their very survival is at stake. Conscious inspiration practice helps sustain that quality of commitment and collectivism through all situations, even under far less dramatic circumstances than founding a group or rescuing it from the brink.

Accountability Reigns

Accountability depends on commitment to a shared purpose and mutually agreed outcomes. This commitment begins with a sense of ownership that flows from an inspiration conversation that integrates the needs, desires, and goals of the individual with those of the group. You will learn much more about accountability in chapter 3. For now, it is enough to know that inspiration is essential in building it.

You Attract the Partners and Resources You Need

Inspiration attracts like-spirited people. Clarity in expressing what you stand for and what your mission is makes it easy for people who share your values and vision to find you—and for you to identify them. Whether they are employees, customers, partners, or donors, they can connect to and support what you're doing. With effective defining stories, and the practices to sustain them that I offer in this chapter, anyone who joins your group will be congruent with "who you are and what you are up to."

Acting Inspired

An organization I worked with badly needed new board members. They were short of the minimum number required by their bylaws and they had no treasurer. The president of the board was particularly frustrated by the difficulty of finding new people. He felt he had talked to everyone he knew and had exhausted all candidates in his small community. While he remained determined, he appeared discouraged and at a loss as to how to attract the people they needed.

As I listened to him, I heard struggle, need, worry, and frustration about how hard things were. In contrast, when I worked on the inspiration element with the full organization, they developed a very lively conversation about their work and crafted a beautiful vision and mission statement. I coached them on speaking from that point of view rather than from a perception of deficit. The president agreed to talk to potential board members about the group's vision for the community rather than its own need for help.

I was delighted to hear the results at my next workshop with the group when the board president told his story. "I was skeptical, but I tried it. I felt foolish at first. But I talked about our vision and what we are working to create, the possibilities we see for the community. And it worked! Three people have joined the board, including the treasurer we desperately needed. This has changed everything in our organization."

The Cost When Inspiration Is Weak

Many of the problems groups struggle with are the result of a lack of story to hold the group together and define what it's doing. Sometimes in my work, the lack of an inspiring story seems to be at the root of *all* the problems an organization faces. Whether or not that's the case, it is certain that without clear purpose and identity—defined in a group's inspiration stories—people are not able to connect their personal ambitions fully to the group or meet their human need for belonging to something larger than themselves.

Let's take a look now at the mirror image of what a strong set of defining stories does for an organization: the image of chaos and dysfunction that result when a group's inspiration is weak or missing altogether.

An inevitable issue that arises when inspiration is missing is what I call *multi-headed beast syndrome*. People tend to go off on whatever track they think might be best, acting as solo operations. They may become distracting, disruptive, or even an impediment to the group's mission. People feel confused as they wonder, "What exactly are we supposed to be accomplishing? How do I know if I'm doing what I should? What is everyone else doing and how does it fit with what I'm supposed to be doing?" In meetings this shows up as "Where is this going? What are we trying to do? What's the point?"

The enterprise is plagued by unfocused, scattered, and disconnected initiatives as people act from their own independent ideas about what is appropriate. People feel isolated and frustrated by wasted efforts, and this feeds a cycle of withdrawal instead of initiative and arbitrary actions instead of actions performed in concert.

Another dynamic that occurs when inspiration is missing is that *control funnels to the top and becomes overcentralized*. People who are not in formal leadership positions are not empowered to act decisively; they can't, because doing so requires clarity of purpose and a sense of certainty that are lacking without defining stories. Some executives may like this state of affairs just fine and use it to serve their personal ambitions, but it doesn't empower the success that groups are truly capable of. Ironically, ambitious leaders who exploit this concentration of power deny themselves the kinds of results that could really make them shine.

A void in the inspiration element allows selfish interests and politics to play out. The result? *Power struggles*. People define what's important in their own terms and grab what they can get. They fight over resources because there is no collectively defined basis for deciding where to direct them. Some individuals use the prevailing lack of clarity as a way to wield personal power. Silos (groups that view themselves independently of the larger group) emerge around anyone with a strong enough vision to attract loyalty. And once silos develop, they are extremely hard to undo.

Another outcome of a void in inspiration is that *controlling personalities can dominate the group*. The defining story known as an identity statement, for example, contains agreements about how the group will conduct itself. If this story is missing, there is no basis on which to check individual behavior. People who have a strong need to dominate or control any situation they are in can and will take hold of the group. Personal agendas prevail over the needs and interests of the many.

Inspiration forms the foundation of accountability, and without it, *accountability flies out the window*. If you have no clarity about what you're creating and how you'll go about it, how can you measure success? What will you hold people accountable *to*, and how will you learn what works and what doesn't?

Groups lacking shared inspiration suffer *disenchantment and disconnection*. This often happens when there is a discrepancy between what people say is important and what they actually do, and it is commonly the consequence of cursory or overly idealistic mission and values statements that do not reflect a genuine group conversation and culture. If the group professes devotion to quality, for example, yet its members continually observe people cutting corners, they will become demoralized, pull back, and disengage. The result is a default culture that doesn't get the full benefit of its people.

The ultimate outcome of all of these destructive forces is that *motivation dies*. Group members experience frustration and discouragement from a lack of accomplishment rooted in fragmentation, competition, and discord. People lose enthusiasm. Dissatisfaction leads to disengagement and withdrawal. Talented people leave—which leads me to the final impact, one guaranteed to contribute to a downward spiral.

It becomes difficult, if not impossible, to attract quality people and resources. Let's face it: who would want to join a group that suffers from such fragmentation and low morale—or contribute to it financially? If you have no unifying, inspiring stories, how can potential employees, donors, stockholders, affiliates, or partners feel confident you can be effective? Perhaps worse, how do you know whom you need to attract and include in your efforts? The danger here is that you are likely to attract people who see your lack of focus and clarity as an opportunity for their own interests to hold sway, and the power struggles and controlling personalities that ensue will only perpetuate your difficulties.

As you can see—and as you have perhaps experienced in groups yourself—most of these problems are interconnected and feed each other once set in motion. They are also resistant to change so it is vital to make sure they do not develop. You can do this by consciously working in inspiration using the tools I provide in this chapter.

If, however, these destructive forces are already at work in your group, don't despair; the same solution applies. Working in inspiration is the necessary first step in beginning the process of transformation into a healthy, productive group. In fact, even when these syndromes are entrenched, a little inspiration work can have a startling impact because people respond dramatically when given the opportunity to connect their personal inspiration with the rest of the group.

Whether you are starting from scratch or working to establish new patterns in your group, the task before you is to build your skills in working with story. The following discussion on the principles of inspiration practice will help you along on that path.

Reflection Questions

1. Is your group energetic and enthusiastic about what it's doing?

2. Is your group engaged in an inspiration conversation that is reflected in written values, vision, mission, and identity statements?

3. Do your members share the same set of core values for your work? Is it evident in the way people talk and behave?

4. Does everyone share the same vision of what your group is creating? Is the vision significant, clear, and compelling enough to keep the team together?

5. Are you confident that everyone in your group is focused on the same purpose and goals?

Principles of Inspiration Practice

Now that you are well acquainted with how inspiration (or the lack of it) shapes a group's capacity for success, and you know that inspiration is created and sustained through story, it's time to begin learning the *how* of the inspiration element of group alchemy. An inspiration practice that captures the full cultural power of story is based on the following principles.

A Word About Leadership

Most leaders are good at tapping into their inspiration on a daily basis—even if they don't call it that. It's one way they become leaders. Part of what we are doing in this chapter is providing awareness of and a language for that ability. In this approach, *leadership* is defined by the capacity to engage people in a shared vision of what is possible and help others tap into it routinely. This means facilitating the group definition of what inspires and empowers each person to play their best part in creating it. The leader then works to help everyone keep the vision alive and active, and engage in renewal and revision when needed.

Principle 1: Inspiration Is Co-Created

The power of an inspiring story is in its authenticity for each member of the group; they can define their personal future in terms of the group's future. This is not a top-down affair. Each person involved in the group must either be part of creating the group's inspiration stories or must intentionally choose to join them when they enter the group.

This is achieved in *conversations that involve everyone*. In large groups, this means engaging all segments of the larger body in creating and renewing the group's inspiration. For newcomers, there must be a recruitment and orientation process that enables them to consciously commit to their place in the organization's story. Without this, you may have vision and mission statements and clear goals and ambitions, but for the most part people will act from their personal ideas, stories, and motivations—as independent agents. While they have joined the group, they have not really joined the *group inspiration*.

Healthy Vision

Mark Laret, CEO at the University of California, San Francisco, embodies this principle in his leadership practice. He was asked to bring the UCSF Medical

Center back to health as it "demerged" from Stanford Medical Center. The organization was losing millions of dollars each year and staff members were demoralized from the upheaval of an unsuccessful merger. Laret knew that it would take a powerful story to galvanize everyone to implement the changes needed to create success. He immediately set about engaging the entire organization in a conversation about the kind of group it could become. He held countless meetings with people across all departments, including regular brown-bag lunch meetings and keeping open office hours. Anyone could talk with him about their concerns and ideas. This also meant that he could speak with each of them personally about the vision he was working from and invite them to join in creating the conversation about what the medical center could become.

Laret has shepherded a massive turnaround: the medical center is profitable, and health outcomes are much improved. He continues to hold open office hours and personally conducts an orientation session for all new employees to discuss the mission of the organization and what it means to be a part of its vision. Despite this success, he still speaks about where the medical center is heading—further vision of what is possible.

Principle 2: Inspiration Is Created and Re-created in Conversations

The best method for engaging everyone in a common purpose and identity is by creating an active conversation, as Mark Laret has done. It is the *experience* of joining with others in that defining conversation that makes it meaningful and personal. Written stories and official statements of vision, mission, goals, and identity are reflections of inspiration, but they are not *it*. They serve as valuable touchstones while the group goes about its daily business, and they serve to communicate its inspiration to the outer world. But it is important not to confuse these statements with inspiration itself. The point is not that you have printed statements you can frame and hang on your wall or publish in your annual report or on your website, but rather that you are having an *ongoing conversation* about your purpose. Then everyone can confidently articulate, understand, and enact your defining stories.

Principle 3: Inspiration Is Explicit

By now it's clear that for everyone to share the same stories of purpose and identity they must be explicit. We cannot take this for granted or assume that everyone shares the same intentions or interpretations. Let's look more closely at why this is so important.

Because stories are fundamental to how we understand and learn, we are always calling them up in order to make sense of what happens around us. This means that there are always many stories operating in any group or culture. When there is no explicit, believable story that shapes our understanding of what's going on, we will make one up. Here's an example of how this works.

Collaboration, Not Control
In offering guidance on how to consciously create the group's stories, I'm not suggesting that you can or should attempt to get "control" of these stories, large or small. Beware. There is a considerable amount of advice around concerning corporate culture that refers to "managing the culture." In the group alchemy method, we recognize that doing so is actually impossible—and that it mistakes control for leadership.

Competing Stories Fracture Groups

Christine was transferred to a different department. This was announced during a staff meeting but no one gave an explanation. It didn't look like a demotion to some, but it occurred during the middle of a big project she was working on so others thought it must be one. Arturo decided it happened because she didn't like her boss in the old department—he always thought that manager was too demanding. Nina decided it was because Christine wasn't doing a good job but the company was too soft to actually fire her. Donald and Samir decided over coffee break that she had personal problems and couldn't put in the overtime that the old job demanded.

In the absence of an explanation for why Christine now sits at a different desk, her coworkers' imaginations have filled in the gap. And the larger and more diversified your group, the more of these kinds of stories there will be.

For instance, the experience of working in the accounting department will be different from that of working in engineering. This might lead to different interpretations and thus different stories about the role of budgeting policies, for example, and how they affect people's ability to do their jobs. Likewise, the experience of working on the board of directors of a small nonprofit is different from the experience of being a program staffer there. The story the directors tell about program changes instituted as a consequence of funding cuts by a major donor might differ substantially from the stories program staff tell about the same situation and what it means to them. The board members might see the organization as a victim of a downturn in the economy. The program staff might see the situation as one in which the board has not done an adequate job of raising funds.

In situations such as these, engaging people in inspiration conversations across groups creates shared stories that provide a unified narrative context for everyone—no matter what subgroup they may belong to.

This is not to say that everyone sees everything the same way. Rather, the personal meanings (expressed in stories) that each member of the group makes up about their experiences will more likely emerge *from that context*. In other words, when you create explicit, collective defining stories, you're helping individuals in the group choose to

A Story Worth Having
Here is one organization's compelling story worth having:

"Water For People works to
build a world where all people
have access to safe drinking
water and sanitation, and where
no one suffers or dies from a
water- or sanitation-related
disease. This is our vision.

"We're on a mission. We
work with people and partners
to develop innovative and
long-lasting solutions to the
water, sanitation, and hygiene
problems in the developing
world. We strive to continually
improve, to experiment with
promising new ideas, and to
leverage resources to multiply
our impact."

create their own empowering stories for their personal experiences as part of the group.

The golden opportunity in conscious inspiration practice is to make sure that the explicit stories we call upon *are genuinely in congruence with our ambitions and what we want to create*.

Principle 4: Inspiration Rests on Expansive Stories Worth Having

While there are lots of stories circulating in any orga-nization, not all of them will empower the group. Some stories are worth having and some are not. It is impor-tant to know the difference between those that serve in-spiration and those that undermine it if you are going to tap into this power to unify and direct our groups. We'll start with the stories you want to build on.

Expansive Stories Worth Having

Stories that serve the group, and thus are worth keeping and tending with care, do the following:

- They name what is possible by describing a future worth working for.
- They articulate the values that make life worth living.
- They define a way of being a group that fulfills people's desire to be part of some-thing bigger than themselves.

Limiting Stories Not Worth Keeping

These kinds of stories do your group a disservice and need to be laid to rest and replaced with expansive stories.

- Stories that define the future in terms of the past.

  "We have always done it this way so that is the way we must do it."
  "The world will always be full of people who …"
- Idealized, inauthentic stories that have little to do with what actually happens in the group.

The CEO speaks regularly about leading an organization that values its people and is committed to respecting employees and customers. Meanwhile, he yells at people and doesn't explain his decisions that affect them, and gossip and backbiting are frequent.

- Haphazard stories without unifying themes and with little consciousness as to their significance.

  Absent a coherent organizational story, each group and department has its own story about what they're doing. If you talk to five different people in the organization, you get a picture of five different companies.

- Neglected stories that do not speak meaningfully to people.

  The organization's mission statement appears on its grant proposals but no one who works there knows what it is. When they read it, it's hard to relate it to what they actually see happening.

It is wise to be alert to the presence of such stories in your group. They create cynicism and break down the group's potential. And they can infect new members when they enter the group, and kill their enthusiasm. Perhaps you have experienced this: you entered a group eager to engage and contribute but over time became discouraged by the negativity and lack of vision. It is very difficult to stay inspired in that situation. Your group's success depends upon expansive stories about what is possible that leave no room for limiting stories.

Inspired Informal Leadership

In group alchemy, everyone can take a leadership role in applying its elements and make a major contribution to the group. If your group doesn't yet have an explicit inspiration conversation, you can begin that discussion. If your group already has vision, mission, and values statements, you can be the one to raise them in conversation to help the group remain inspired when facing a big decision or challenge. Your personal practice of staying focused on your inspiration can help others do so. Your own modeling of inspiration will be contagious; people are hungry for it, and they usually respond energetically to the spark.

This practice is up to the individual, of course. We cannot force others to choose to be inspired. We can, however, create the conditions that facilitate and encourage them to do so. This is the role of leadership, and it is the role of the habits in the group.

Principle 5: Inspiration Is a Continual Choice

If we squander all our attention on what is wrong, we will miss the prize:
In the chaos engulfing the world, a hopeful future resides because the past is
disintegrating before us. If that is difficult to believe, think about winter;
calculate what it requires to create a single springtime.
—Paul Hawken

To be uncommonly successful, we must claim our vision of what we care most about and return to it every day, in everything we do. In this way, inspiration means *choosing to be inspired*: this means taking a stand to stay focused on what we are committed to and continually recommitting to that.

The world can appear full of possibility or full of problems. Each perspective yields different results. It's easy to get focused on obstacles in our way or reasons why something *can't* happen. When we do, our attention and energy can quickly become defined by struggle. When we get stuck on that track, we have lost our sense of what is possible and instead re-create our experience as what's wrong. We are in danger of losing touch with all the energy and enthusiasm that exist in our inspiration stories. Quality and productivity suffer.

Consider the times when you have felt most energized and engaged in a project or task. I'm sure you will find an inspired state of mind at the center of that time. Creating and re-creating your vision in the world is intrinsically enlivening. It becomes magnetic and people want to join you in it.

It is vital to develop a habit of noticing when you are focused on problems rather than possibilities, recognizing when you experience a burden rather than enthusiasm, and choosing to place your attention on your inspiration—and then to act from that as reality. How do you accomplish this? By continually asking, "What inspires me? What change in the world could I see because I was here, doing this, today?" When you go into a meeting, ask yourself and the group, "What are we doing this for? What can we accomplish here that will get us closer to our vision?"

Principle 6: Inspiration Is a Group Custom

Group inspiration depends not just upon personal habits and discipline but also upon habits *in the group*. These are practices that help everyone become reinspired by routinely calling up what you have committed to creating together. I call these *customs* because they are practiced in the group and they work to create the culture.

Inspiration is ultimately about how our dreams and aspirations shape what we *do*. It is not enough to have a powerful story; everything you say and do within your group must retell that story and inspire others with it. This means that inspiration cannot be a static thing—*it exists in action.* When inspiration stories are alive in a group, they can be heard in everyday talk and seen in how the work gets done.

Group practices of inspiration remind people of their personal conviction and the meaning the group's purpose holds for them. They make it easier to stay focused and on track—together. And they can create their vision, just as the mason creates his cathedral.

With this in mind, we can look more closely at how you can create the habits and customs that will keep your group connected to your inspiration and energetically creating the results you have identified together as most important.

Practices for Powerful Inspiration

If your group already exists then you will want to begin with an assessment of your inspiration. If your group is new then you can go right to the second practice to create your inspiration.

Assess the State of Your Group's Inspiration

Groups that have been around for a while need to determine whether they are engaged in an inspiring conversation that connects everyone. The following questions and exercises can help.

1. Do you all share an overarching story about "who you are and what you are up to," or are there many disparate stories in your group?
2. Are you working from a story you chose or one that you inherited?
3. Are your members personally inspired by your group's vision and mission?
4. If each group member were asked to name the top organizational priorities, would the answers be the same?
5. Can each member relate their personal responsibilities to the organization's mission?

You might use some or all of the following activities to help you answer these questions:

- Ask each other to say or write your own versions of your group's vision and mission. Discuss them together. Do you share the same understanding of the mission?
- Conduct an exercise in which everyone relates their personal responsibilities to the organization's mission or to the goals of the team.
- Use the questions in this chapter and summarized in appendix A to conduct a group assessment. This can be a discussion, a focus group, a questionnaire, a series of interviews, or any combination that makes sense for the size and composition of your group.

Create Your Inspiring Conversations and Statements

If you are forming a new group or determine that your existing group lacks strong inspiration stories, you will need to create them. This is the place to start when embarking on any shared endeavor; I do this with all my clients, work partners, consultants—anyone with whom I will be working on a shared outcome. Sometimes this can be handled in an informal, brief conversation; sometimes it requires a formal retreat. The important thing is to allow time for people to shift into a creative mind-set and communicate openly. The kind of setting and amount of time you devote to this depends on your intentions and the size and history of the group.

Begin with Personal Reflection

It is a good idea to give everyone a chance to get off autopilot for a few minutes and think about their personal goals and aspirations in relation to the group, the job, or the project. We often are not fully aware of what we want so it is important for each person to get clear about what they need to have reflected in the group and what they want from it. This is the conscious engagement that really links individual ambitions with collective purpose. You can use these questions to help:

What moves you to take action in your life? What do you care most about?
How can you connect powerfully with the purpose of the group you are in?

The answers to these questions are your inspiration. Personal power comes from answering them consciously and matching them with actions.

Personal Practice

- Decide that you will live from a standpoint that your vision can become real. Break your focus on problems and limitations. Act as though that future exists now. Find what works for you personally to do this. Is it a daily meditation? Or perhaps you find it helpful to work with a personal coach. Maybe journaling or reviewing personal affirmations work for you. The key is to see the specific things you can do each day to bring your inspiration into focus.

- Own your inspiration. Learn to speak from your vision. Practice so you can do so in your own words. Work with people outside your team or organization to help you find your own inspiring voice. Take inspiration from the board president I mentioned
earlier who was able to recruit all the board members he needed once he started speaking from his inspiration.

Create Your Vision and Values Statements

Define what you are committed to creating in the world, what the authors of *Tribal Leadership* describe as your "noble cause." As you do this you will also identify the underlying core values that unite you.

A true vision of the world we want is powerful. It can also be daunting because we are so enmeshed in the way things are now that it is often difficult to disentangle and see other possibilities. Provide for a process that can help people think creatively and expansively. Very practically minded people sometimes get impatient with this practice because the visions that arise can seem unrealistic compared to present reality. If this happens, just remind them that the practical considerations will come next.

You can access more visioning tips at www.groupalchemy.net/vision.

Create Your Mission and Goal Statements

Your mission is your path toward the world you are creating. You might share a vision of the world with other groups, but your particular mission will be distinct to your group. For instance, there might be many health care groups that share a vision of a world where everyone has health care. But your mission might be to provide primary health care to low-income members of the community while another organization might have a mission to provide state-of-the-art cardiac care.

Make sure that your goals are aligned with your mission, that they are strategic, and that they are specific and measurable. How will you know whether you're succeeding if you can't measure your results and make the adjustments you need?

Create Your Identity Statements

As a group or organization, who do you need to be—how do you need to act together—in order to accomplish your mission? This element is often overlooked. Yet this is where the people in the group actually live: where they need to be able to say what is important for them to be fully engaged and productive group members. What does it mean in your group to respect each other? What will be the protocol for sharing ideas and discussing different views? Are you charged up by intense debate or do you perform better with calm, moderated discussion? This will become a crucial foundation for the agreements that structure your work, the subject of the next chapter.

Create Inspiration Touchstones

Inspiration doesn't take root just because you held a meeting to create a vision and mission statement. You need to reinvest in it repeatedly. Keeping inspiration an active force in the group depends on ways to teach, practice, institutionalize, and publicly praise contributions to your values, vision, and mission.

Both routine and spontaneous moments are valuable. Some possibilities include:

Hold "mission moments." This might mean beginning a meeting with a short story about a recent event that illustrates acting on your values and mission. Or read the mission statement at the beginning of a meeting. Use storytelling. These could be product demonstrations, case studies, success stories, or compelling first-hand presentations. You can read your inspiration statements aloud. Put them in song, or rap, or poems. Role-play enacting your values. Choose whatever works to ignite the passion they represent in your group.

Structure meetings around mission and goals. Make sure that topics are discussed in terms of their role in moving your mission and goals forward, not as abstract issues.

Make your values and mission explicit in your decision-making process. You might keep your mission posted on the wall to refer to while making decisions. Make sure your values and goals are part of any decision rubrics you use.

Post inspiring stories. Post statements, diagrams, pictures, or anything that represents what you stand for and your successes in the office: on a meeting agenda, in emails—wherever they will inspire people. Change them often to refresh this visual cue and keep it alive.

Appoint "mission keepers." Have someone take a special role for keeping the mission in front. Rotate this function.

Do things that inspire you. My clients usually list professional development and other learning experiences as important activities they find inspiring.

Keep the personal connected to the group. Find out what motivates and inspires each member of the group and help them stay in touch with it. Create ways to help each member meet their personal goals and needs.

Attract inspired people. The point of entry into your group is an inspiration touchstone. Make your inspiration an explicit part of your hiring (or board selection) process so you attract people who are inspired by your vision and mission and who intentionally choose to join you in them. Then orient new people to the practices you use that keep your inspiration alive.

Intentional reinforcements such as these provide group members a chance to re-experience the spirit of purpose that gives meaning and provides context for what they and their fellow members are doing.

Periodically Reassess Your Inspiration

In the pressure of everyday challenges, multiple distractions, and competing interests, it's easy to get pulled out of your inspiration. So periodically taking stock of the health of your group's inspiration will help you make sure that you aren't neglecting this element of your success. Consider creating a routine structure for the following:

Assess whether your inspiration is still compelling to the people in your group. Do your formal written statements still reflect the conversation that inspires your group? Does everyone still share the same story for what you're up to? Do people find it easy to choose to be inspired about what you're doing? Use the appropriate assessment questions in appendix A to help you with this.

Evaluate the consistency between words and actions. It's not uncommon for formal values or vision statements to differ from what people actually do. Our project here is to build a culture that supports success. It will not work if there are systemic breaks from your stated inspiration. You need to know what is true in your group.

Make an assessment of your culture and how it relates to your stated ideals. Are you still focused on your core mission or have you let your focus drift? If you say you value quality, do you encourage people to take the time to do a high-quality job, or do you stress budgetary containment so much that people overlook problems with quality? Are your goals structuring your work, or do people work on whatever they feel is important at the time?

Reassessment Questions

Following are some questions to ask about your inspiration and your actions, and whether they match.
1. Have you defined your organizational structure, policies, and procedures to be in line with your inspiration? Can you clearly see your values expressed throughout all of these areas?
2. Do you have pockets in your organization where the declared values and vision are not being practiced?

3. Have you hired people who share your values? Do you have a hiring process in place to ensure that new hires understand your vision and mission and see themselves in it? Do you make it clear what is expected in this regard?

4. Have you trained people in their jobs in ways that makes it possible for them to live your values?

5. Are you routinely assessing your work in terms of your values and mission?

Be honest in this; neither denial nor wishful thinking will serve you. You might need some outside perspective. You can ask your customers, clients, community partners, evaluators, and organizational consultants to help you assess your real culture. If you haven't been conscious of this, you may find that you've been up to something different than you thought.

We all know that sometimes there is a difference between what people say and what they do. None of us is perfect. The key is to learn to identify those instances and make the choice to return to integrity.

Be True to Your Inspiration

The places where you see gaps between what you say you value and what is actually happening are opportunities to spark your inspiration. You can quickly make a quantum leap forward in achieving your goals by simply aligning your actions with your stated inspiration. Making the necessary changes, whether by adjusting your actions or changing your words and formal inspiration statements to fit what's actually happening, involves the accountability and honesty that are critical to maintaining inspiration and achieving your goals. We will look at this more deeply in the chapter on accountability.

Celebrate, Extend, and Renew Your Inspiration

Don't take your inspiration for granted. Periodically check in: "Is everyone excited about what we're doing here? Does everyone share the same vision of what is possible?" If the response is less than enthusiastic, do something to reinspire and activate the vision.

Expand on what works. Have a discussion about what's worked and what hasn't for keeping your inspiration active. This might occur as part of a strategic planning process or a visioning retreat. Periodically holding these kinds of formal conversations helps refresh the group's inspiration and update its stories as circumstances change. Then you can institutionalize more of what works and stop doing things that detract.

Practice acknowledgment. Take the time to speak to a coworker to acknowledge him for a specific contribution he made recently. Publicly praise people for the job they're doing. We will look more closely at acknowledgment and its role in inspiration in the chapter on that element.

Connect with your customers (clients, patients, partners, etc.) to hear and feel the difference you are making.

Hold special events. Include a wide swath of stakeholders in your inspiration conversations by holding an awards banquet, a conference, or a community project.

Finally, it is worth remembering to remain committed but not attached; that is, hold a firm but flexible grip on your commitments. Changes in circumstances, including the achievement of success, can change what is possible and how you go about achieving it. Learning and adaptability are stifled by a mindless attachment to a predefined end or expectation; inflexibility is contrary to inspiration.

Inspiration: Lessons Learned

The organization that wins in the twenty-first century will focus its attention on passion. It will find, develop, and articulate a vision for which all of its people will be willing to fight long and hard.
—James Lucas, *The Passionate Organization*

The alchemy in powerful groups occurs because they create conscious, explicit stories about their purpose and identity that serve to align desire with the energy to create. They keep that inspiration present in their ongoing conversations so that the collective inspiration connects to each member's personal passion. They establish practices that keep that passion alive. And if their stories no longer serve, they deliberately change them. They don't let unconscious, contrary stories creep in and take over.

Everyone in your organization is creating their own stories and recalling their own versions of shared stories. Even though you cannot control all the stories in your group, you can create a cultural environment, based on explicitly shared stories, that encourages positive interpretations and choices from everyone.

Together the practices outlined in this chapter can become the customs that support this kind of inspiration in your group. As your purpose and values infuse everything you do and continually animate the group, members will remain inspired to give their absolute best effort to the group enterprise. They will be moved to find ways to continue their work together even when doing so is challenging and the outcome is uncertain. With the integration of inspiration practices, the process of group alchemy has begun.

It's easy to overlook the importance of inspiration, especially in the rush to get things done and deal with the urgent needs in front of us. Some dismiss the very idea as "soft" and perfunctorily produce the required mission statement so they can move on to the "real work." Or, inspiration is thought of as something individuals must generate for themselves. Our society encourages this, with its emphasis on the rational and practical over the emotional and symbolic. As this chapter draws to a close, we now know that this is a serious mistake. It denies us the opportunity to tap into the passion of the group and empower everyone to be full participants.

The human capacity for accomplishment is immense. We see this often in what people of little means do for their children, fighting against the odds to provide opportunity and protect them from anything that might limit their success. We see it in people prevailing against adversity to grow their businesses. Their inspiration is clear, and it fuels their capacity. We can learn from their examples.

Providing Practical Structure for Inspiration

Inspiration is the beginning. Turning that inspiration into consistent collaboration that gets results involves the other five elements of group alchemy. The next step in this process is to structure your work around your inspiration with powerful agreements, the subject of the next chapter.

Resources

Community, Peter Block, Barrett-Koehler, San Francisco, 2008

Tribal Leadership: Leveraging Natural Groups to Build a Thriving Organization, David Logan, John King and Halee Fischer-Wright, New York: Collins, 2008.

The Passionate Organization: Igniting the Fire of Employee Commitment, James R. Lucas, AMACOM, NY, 1999.

Element Two:

Agreements

Establish clarity and efficiency

Build trust

Harness possibility

Make fair agreements and stick to them.
—Confucius

The group's inspiration is your guiding light, the North Star that generates a spirit of what is possible and sets a course for your success. But once you're united and energized, how will your work get done? Organizing people and coordinating activities is the job of *agreements*.

We are all used to making agreements—we do it all the time. We might agree to get together at 3 p.m. to discuss our project. Or I might hire a marketing manager and she will agree to perform certain tasks and reach specific goals by the end of the year. In most cases, it's as simple as that. But not always.

It may surprise you that most of us are unaware of the many agreements that operate in our groups and how they determine what can happen. This chapter will help you understand the different kinds of agreements in groups and the roles they play in any group's success. It also offers valuable practices that show you how to create the kinds of strong agreements that will enable you to access the full power of this element of group alchemy.

The agreements task of powerful groups is to develop strong, explicit agreements that support your commitment to your inspiration.

Structuring Your Work Together

All social groups must organize themselves and coordinate their members' activities. Since humans first used language, we have had the ability to negotiate these kinds of arrangements. We don't have to fight it out; we can talk it through and reach *agreement*.

Agreements are essentially arrangements made between two or more people concerning a course of action. All social interactions and relationships depend on agreements. They make up the "rules of the game." I like to call these the *scaffolding* that forms the structure for the group and its work. They serve to define relationships and establish what constitutes acceptable behavior. In this way agreements harmonize people's expectations of each other.

When consciously formed, agreements give groups the power to act in accordance with their values and aims. When formed *unconsciously*, however, as they often are, with little or only fleeting thought, they can wreak havoc on a group. I will have more to say about this later, but first let's look at the alchemical promise of strong, effective agreements.

The Alchemy of Conscious Agreements

Following are the invaluable effects of powerful agreements.

Clarity and Confidence

Agreements coordinate actions and help reduce confusion and uncertainty. By making explicit agreements, we can avoid breakdowns in communication caused by operating from differing assumptions, as well as the resentment and distrust that follow such breakdowns.

Collaboration and Full Participation

It is in the shadows created by a lack of explicitness in agreements that manipulation and power plays occur. Conscious agreements can eliminate the politics that plague many organizations and marginalize some people at the hands of others. The result is that everyone has the opportunity to participate.

Responsibility and Accountability

We have a sense of ownership and responsibility for agreements that we make, and this sense is the necessary basis for accountability. We will look at this in more depth throughout this chapter and in the next chapter on accountability.

Trust

Trust comes from keeping agreements. When other people follow through on what they have agreed to do, we learn to trust them. And of course others learn to trust us, too, when they continually observe that we keep our part of the bargain. It becomes a positive feedback loop of agreeing to a course of action, seeing our expectations of others met, and developing greater certainty that this will continue to happen. And the more trust that is generated in this way, the easier it is to raise concerns and make adjustments or new agreements when needed.

The Ability to Address Performance Breakdowns and Unproductive Behavior

When an active conversation that is rooted in the inspiration process described in the last chapter is present, the group can make agreements about "who we want to be as a group." Then, if it becomes necessary to address a behavior that doesn't work, it's a matter of calling the person back to the agreement that she or he made. This takes much of the charge out of a situation that might otherwise lead to conflict, and can dramatically reduce defensiveness and resistance.

The Strength of a Reminder

A client I'll call Helen phoned me one afternoon extremely frustrated by the lack of initiative and follow-through on the part of one of her employees, Alan. It was causing a big disruption to their workflow. We had recently held a staff retreat where we had worked together on inspiration and agreements about the staff culture they wanted to create. Helen was discouraged that after we had gone to all this effort, Alan's behavior was still a problem. We discussed how she could speak to him from the perspective of the agreements he had committed to at the retreat along with everyone else. She was game. She explained to him how his behavior was affecting her and the group, and pointed out that it wasn't consistent with what he had committed to.

Because he had been part of the conversation that created agreements about what they all wanted from each other, Alan was able to listen to this feedback without getting defensive. He could see her point, and he recalled his own participation in arriving at the agreement. He responded very positively and his work performance increased dramatically right away.

Reducing the Effects of Personality on the Group

Behavioral agreements, a category we will discuss in the Principles of Agreement Practice section of this chapter, provide the mechanisms for ensuring appropriate levels of participation and restraint and are an effective way to address the influence of personality on groups. Agreements can be used to prevent small distractions or address larger problems of bullying and controlling behavior.

The Cost When Agreements Are Weak

You may recognize some of these telltale signs that agreements are weak—or missing altogether.

Uncertainty and confusion abound. Being in a group without strong agreements is like trying to play in a symphony without a musical score or a conductor. You don't know what part to play, when to come in, when to stop, or how loudly to play. The result is noise, not music.

Distrust and wariness build as creativity wanes. It's not uncommon to have the appearance of an agreement—people nodding their heads during a meeting—that then breaks down when one or more people fail to keep it because they never actually made an explicit commitment. (Silence or lack of dissent does not equal agreement!) If agreements are weak because of a lack of commitment and integrity (heads nodding so people appear cooperative while they're inwardly saying, "No way!"), there is no basis from which to trust individuals or the group to craft good agreements that stick. This generally puts people on guard; unsure of what they can really count on, they assume a defensive posture. Such an atmosphere stifles creativity and can become highly toxic.

Multi-headed beast syndrome rules the day. Recall our multi-headed beast from chapter 1. There is more than one way this can happen in groups; lack of agreement creates the same effect. In the absence of powerful agreements, everyone is left to operate from their own assumptions and inferences—essentially operating in their own worlds. If those worlds don't happen to coincide, misunderstandings and conflict result. People go their respective ways and silos develop.

The group loses needed capabilities. As assumptions and expectations go unmet, frustration and conflict grow. The group ends up covering the same ground over and over again, wasting time and energy. The synergistic benefit of people working together is lost. Over time, some people disengage, hold back their contributions, withdraw, and give in to resignation. Others cope with this unsatisfying dynamic by attempting to manipulate and dominate the situation, either to get what they want or even just to feel secure that things are under control.

Personalities increasingly dominate the group. Without clear behavioral agreements that people can be held accountable to, dominating personalities take charge and work to exert control over the group. They are able to act without boundaries and with impunity. Down that road lies chaos.

Who's in Charge?

Here's a story that exemplifies many of these problems. Some version of this scenario is quite common and always presents a problem for group effectiveness.

A teacher described to me her experience of her school's faculty meetings. "One guy loves to hear himself talk. He constantly butts in while someone else is talking. Literally—he jumps in with 'but, but, but ...' then takes the floor and goes on and on. I watch people roll their eyes, obviously fed up. No one says anything—the principal never does anything. But after the meeting everybody gossips about it and how much time we wasted. Everybody thinks he's totally obnoxious."

By not addressing this situation the group continues to waste time—time that could be used productively to further the mission of the group—and people feel frustrated and dread meetings. The group's enthusiasm is deflated every time they meet. Listening to this teacher, I heard a sense of helplessness about how to do anything to repair the situation and make meeting time more productive.

Agreements about which kinds of behavior are acceptable and which are not, how to conduct meetings, and how to handle situations that aren't productive would give this group the foundation for dealing with such unproductive behavior and empower everyone in the group to address it; even the language the group used to discuss the matter would change. Rather than a complaint based on the opinion that "he's obnoxious," the situation could be phrased as "that behavior does not support our success." The situation moves out of the typical realm of criticizing personality to a matter of being in integrity with inspiration commitments and agreements, which takes the wind out of defensive responses.

The Kinds of Agreements Groups Have

All groups have their own version of the following kinds of agreements. As I describe these, see if you can identify them in your group. When you learn to recognize them, you can make sure your agreements are strong ones.

Agreements Address either Structural or Behavioral Issues

It's helpful to group the types of agreements into two categories.

Agreements about Structure

Agreements about structure organize people in terms of relationship, roles, responsibility, and power. This is often reflected visually in an organizational chart that describes who has authority and accountability in a given area, and who reports to whom. When you accept a job in an organization, you are entering into a structural agreement.

The group's vision, mission, and goals also serve as agreements about structure in that they organize people around what to do. Organizational policies are included in this category because they serve to create the structure for what can and cannot be done.

Culture Note: Newbies
and the Struggle to Fit In
All groups operate with a whole
host of implicit agreements.
Because they usually lie outside
our awareness, we don't even
realize we are applying them
and expecting others to do the
same.

This is why joining a group
can be so difficult. As a new-
comer, we have to expend a lot
of time and effort watching for
and learning the hidden agreements, figuring out what these
underlying rules are and trying
to behave accordingly. The
silver lining is that as humans,
we are masters at learning unspoken agreements; we've been
practicing since we were babies!
Still, we can rapidly increase the
pace at which people become
effective and productive members of the group if we develop
awareness in this area, make
those unspoken agreements
explicit, and develop orientation programs that introduce
newcomers to the agreements
of the group. Find out how
further along in Practices for
Powerful Agreements.

Agreements about Conduct

What I call *agreements about conduct* outline "how
we do things around here" by defining what counts
as appropriate behavior. Some of these are formal,
such as an official code of conduct, or an agreement
about how a decision will be made, or even—though
it may seem counterintuitive—a formal agreement to
have "casual Fridays." They can also be informal and
less consciously created. An example would be when
people fall into a habit of sharing stories about what
they did over the weekend before the official Monday-
morning staff meeting. In this case, there is a tacit
agreement that this is an accepted activity for that
time and place.

When you consider the range of agreements operating in our groups, workplaces, and society as a
whole, summarized in table 1, I think you can see why
I refer to them as scaffolding that shapes our actions.
Each item includes examples of what such agreements
might entail.

Agreements Can Be Explicit or Implicit

Just as it is important to recognize the two categories of agreements—structural and behavioral—it is
equally important to see that both types can operate
on two different levels: explicit or implicit (hidden).
By learning to spot the difference, your group can consistently make strong agreements that work for you instead of against you.

Explicit Agreements: Let There Be No Doubts

We usually use the word agreement to refer to something explicitly stated, so it's easy to
understand this level of agreement. Explicit agreements are by definition clearly communicated. The best ones are specific, unambiguous, and easy to navigate.

Explicit agreements may be verbal, such as "I will have that report to you by the end
of the day today" or "We will go to the conference together." They may also be written
down, perhaps in a policy and procedures manual or an employee handbook. Your job

Table 1: The kinds of agreements that shape what happens in groups

Agreements about Structure

Purpose: vision, mission, and goals

Composition: who is, or needs to be, in the group including criteria such as skill set, experience, knowledge of issues, and demographic representation

Organization:

- Functions: what activities need to be accomplished by whom, such as leader, facilitator, treasurer

- Roles: who takes up each function

- Groups: departments/committees/special task forces

Power and leadership: distribution of rights and responsibilities

Time: schedules and how time will be used

Modes of communication: reports, meetings, email, etc.

Agreements about Conduct

Rules of conduct: what counts as acceptable behavior such as the level of formality or informality, use of technology in meetings, when to share information, and the like

Communication: how discussions are conducted, what respectful talk means, whether multiple people speaking at the same time is acceptable, intensity of argumentation that is acceptable

Meeting processes: facilitation methods, use of agenda, note taking, roles

Problem-solving methods: choice of using hypothesis testing, root cause analysis, or other methods

Decision making: who will decide and how—by consensus, voting, discussion followed by leader deciding?

Working with conflict: methods for handling conflict, such as mediation

Learning: approaches to new situations and problems, commitments to learning-and-development programs

description is an explicit structural agreement between you and your employer. Dress codes, rules about email protocol, and ground rules that your group uses during meetings are all explicit behavioral agreements.

Implicit Agreements: Your Guess May Not Be as Good as Mine

Another type of agreement that is equally important but that operates outside of awareness is the implicit kind. These differ from assumptions because *they are held collectively*, though not expressed openly. No one tells you directly what you must do or not do but you learn these rules just the same, and quickly, when you join the group because you see them expressed in the ways people behave. They are equally important rules of the game.

Norms Are Agreements

Unspoken rules of conduct are called *norms,* a term that simply refers to broad cultural agreements that serve as taken-for-granted rules about what counts as appropriate behavior. By coordinating behavior, they create a comfort zone so that we can all relax and go about our business without having to continually negotiate every decision.

While the word norm generally applies here, I use the term *agreement* instead in order to stress the fact that *when we act in accordance with these subtle rules we are in fact agreeing to this code of conduct.* Recognizing this means that we can take responsibility for agreements of this kind. They need not be taken for granted or treated as inevitable.

While we may be conscious of some of these implicit agreements, many of them are outside our regular awareness so we don't recognize them as agreements at all. Nonetheless, when we act in accordance with them we are acting "in agreement."

Your group might operate with an implicit agreement that laughter and joking are part of what makes being in the group worthwhile, and this agreement will serve to create and maintain bonds among group members. Or some of these examples may sound familiar: "Don't bring up subjects that could appear to criticize something someone in the group is doing." "Show drafts of your work while it's in development" or the reverse— "Don't reveal your work until it's complete and you're ready to make a final presentation." "It's okay to check email and to text during meetings." "Don't disagree with the boss" is a common implicit agreement. "Don't talk about uncomfortable topics" is another common one.

Implicit Agreements Develop Automatically

Many of the agreements about conduct that prescribe how people act are in the implicit category, and this happens naturally. It is in the nature of social groups that as people come together and interact routinely, they automatically develop rules for how to behave. These are often unspoken because they develop organically through interactions. Consider humor in the workplace and accepted attire. All it takes is a critical look or a cool response to a joke, particularly by someone in authority, and the joking will stop. If a male member of the group decides not to wear a tie one day and no one reacts negatively, others may follow his example until it becomes common for men to leave their ties at home.

Warning: Some of Your Agreements May be Hazardous to Your Success!

The fact is that more and more implicit agreements develop in groups over time through the push-pull of personalities trying to get what they want. As people work to accommodate, influence, or dominate each other through routine interactions, conversations, and meetings, the group increasingly acts based on undeclared, unexpressed, taken-for-granted agreements about how things work and how everyone should behave. *An entire culture develops without anyone saying a word about its rules.*

And herein lies the rub. While many implicit agreements are harmless or even help the group function, many do not serve the group. Because their effects have not been openly considered, they can be very detrimental.

As an example, let's look at a simple situation that is extremely common: sloppy start times for meetings. I have seen some version of the following happen countless times.

"What Time Is Ten O'clock?"

There is a weekly staff meeting scheduled for 10:00 a.m. Several people are there just before 10:00. Other people gradually trickle in over the next five or ten minutes. One or two walk into the meeting room and put a folder down where they want to sit, look around and see that the meeting hasn't started yet and go back out—maybe to get a cup of coffee or retrieve something from their office or make a quick phone call. There is casual discussion amongst pairs or small groups of people sitting around the table, waiting. Finally someone, usually but not always the formal leader, says something like "Okay, let's get started." It's 10:10. Or 10:17 or 10:20. It varies each week and it is often difficult to identify what triggers the actual beginning of the meeting.

What's happening here is that people in the group are not keeping an agreement to start the meeting at 10 a.m. This means that they are not being accountable for the agreement that they have made. (I'll have much more to say about the particular qualities of accountability in the next chapter.)

And there is more to it than that. There are also *implicit agreements in force:* "It's okay to be late," "A little time wasted here and there is not a problem," and "There's only one person with the authority to get this meeting started" are some of the conclusions meeting participants might draw about the unwritten code of behavior in this group.

It's important to realize that when explicit agreements are broken, whatever accommodations take place often become implicit agreements. This means you have essentially *slipped into an agreement that may not be serving the needs of the group.* Until someone in the group raises the question about whether that practice is meeting your needs, you cannot tap into the full potential of your group.

This issue of when meetings begin is often treated as a trivial matter. Some people think it's considerate to wait for group members who are late getting to the meeting. Others see strong agreements about punctuality as overly compulsive or controlling. And some might see tardiness or casual start times as disrespectful while others think it's no big deal either way.

So who is "right?" Which of the possible interpretations is accurate? *Who knows?* This is precisely the kind of diversity that exists in groups and why conscious discussion and agreements that explore and resolve differences in assumptions and ideas are essential.

My research indicates that effectiveness and success arise from predictable, trustworthy agreements that allow people to efficiently coordinate their actions. I have not seen it achieved through unilateral action that allows everyone to make their own interpretations about how agreements apply to them individually.

Consider the deeper implications of the kinds of hidden agreements that have developed in the story I just shared. Because there is a consistent discrepancy between a stated agreement and what actually happens, potentially more destructive agreements develop. "What we say is not what we mean" and "We don't have to keep our agreements" are dangerous agreements to establish, with the potential to undermine even explicit agreements.

Now apply this perspective to other situations, such as variability in quality of work or ambiguity about completion of projects in a timely manner, and you can see what a slippery slope this can be. These kinds of unresolved differences can feed an attitude of distrust and a lack of confidence. This is where cynicism breeds. Which agreements are to be kept and which do not matter? What should I believe? How can I trust? It's not hard to see how corrosive this is to people's ability to work powerfully together. Everyone is left to make their own interpretations and choose their own level of responsiveness.

You can avoid this by simply uncovering the implicit agreements that are in your way and negotiating explicit agreements that match your intentions and inspiration. The rest of this chapter shows you how to go about doing that in a way that will truly tap into the power in your group.

Reflection Questions

1. Can you identify the agreements about structure and conduct that exist in your group?

2. Does everyone share the same understanding of each other's roles?

3. Are your goals explicit agreements, clearly stating what you will do, who will do it, and by when?

4. Do you have clear, explicit agreements about *how* you are going to work together as a group?

5. Where are there friction points in your group that might indicate where you need to refine your agreements?

6. Can you identify a time when someone brought up counterproductive behavior in order to establish explicit agreements that support your group's effectiveness? Does everyone feel free to do so as needed?

Principles of Agreement Practice

As with inspiration practices, there is a set of principles that will guide you in developing alchemy in the agreement element.

Principle 1: Strong Agreements Are Explicit

This is where the full power of agreements lies, in developing them consciously, explicitly, and intentionally. Hidden agreements can be terribly arbitrary and are often a product of particular personalities.

Here's an example of how these kinds of hidden agreements can develop over time: When a group first forms, everyone openly shares their ideas and engages in wide-ranging discussion to vet them. Then a couple of people in the group start letting loose with scathing criticism of some of the ideas presented. The more soft-spoken and sensitive people recoil from this, gradually pull back, and decide to withhold their thoughts while the more competitive and noisy members dominate the discussions. In this case, the agreement has developed that it's all right to shout over people and to "fight it out" by critically putting down other people's ideas. Though its numbers may not decrease at first, because this agreement is in place, the group has effectively shrunk because it is no longer getting the benefit of everyone's expertise. Eventually some members will leave in search of a less hostile environment.

Something like this happened in one executive group I worked with. The new CEO asked me to help with what he experienced as a very difficult group. I will describe this at length because I think it illustrates a very important aspect of what can happen in groups that cause them to lose their effectiveness.

Execs Get Explicit

As I worked with this executive group to negotiate agreements for its meetings, we ended up in a long discussion about whether or not it was okay for people to interrupt and talk over others. It surprised me how long it took to get some of the more aggressive talkers to hear those who found the meetings to be what they called "painful" and that they felt they were not being heard. The strongly held viewpoints about what worked or what didn't work in meetings and the distinctly different experiences became clear. Several people, including the CEO, said they found it hard even to think at times during their weekly meetings. Others said that they thought everyone got through eventually and that they enjoyed the intense back-and-forth. They wanted to be able to do just as they pleased.

It became clear that the group was operating with an implicit agreement along the lines of "It's okay to interrupt and talk over other people as long as what I'm

saying is relevant to our discussion and I think it's important (and I'm right)."
Note that even though the more soft-spoken members did not like this, they had
acquiesced to the more assertive talkers, at a loss for what to do to change things.

A pointed discussion (with some assertive facilitation!) was necessary before
the more aggressive group could even hear that there was a problem. But once
they did they were able to reach some different agreements and the entire atmosphere changed. Their meetings became calmer and more orderly. Everyone felt
they had a chance to be heard; there was a striking expression of courtesy and
willingness to turn the floor over to the more soft-spoken members.

Granted, the more aggressive talkers had to adjust to a slower pace than they
liked at times, and initially there were some jokes about raising hands. But in
quick order a new meeting style developed where everyone's contributions were
considered more carefully—a tremendous benefit to the group's efficacy. Over time
the group became confident that they were able to reach better decisions because
they had the benefit of more information and different points of view. And people
began to enjoy the meetings more.

This experience taught me just how important and how challenging this matter of
implicit agreements can be. In this group, there was an underlying agreement to let the
more assertive or domineering people hold sway. Their willingness to impose their argumentation style on everyone is a good example of the fact that implicit agreements are
often the reflection of the most domineering persons in the group. And they were not
trying to be rude or difficult. I think they all genuinely respected each other. In their
highly competitive culture, they simply did not (or didn't want to) see their style as a
problem.

The opposite situation could be equally problematic for a group's effectiveness. If the
culture in the group has developed around passivity, or avoidance of conflict at all cost,
then the constructive friction that leads to challenges to the status quo and valuable new
ideas might not be allowed. Then the group has sacrificed results for the sake of feeling
good.

Either situation means that the group is personality driven rather than results driven. And
a personality-driven group is fundamentally weak; it can sabotage its own success by
deviating from the group's defining stories and thereby drain the inspiration from the
group. Remember, that's when people begin to withdraw, so the personality-driven group
misses the benefit of the full capabilities of everyone in the group as some people become
silenced.

Furthermore, in the laissez-faire, low-accountability culture driven by implicit
agreements, it's easy for people to say yes to something even when they're not truly com-

mitted. This siphons off much of the group's potential. The environment of uncertainty and defensiveness and the loss of inspired participation feed much of the struggle in groups that ultimately destroys their power.

You do not have to suffer this loss of performance in your group. If implicit agreements can be the enemy of effectiveness, the answer lies in creating strong agreements that work.

Principle 2: Strong Agreements Are Specific

For agreements to support effective action, they need to clearly convey their meaning to everyone involved. This is often not as simple as it sounds.

Not all explicitly stated agreements are equally effective. Many suffer from a lack of clarity and specificity. (We could say they are not explicit *enough*.) It is quite common for people to think they have made an agreement, only to find out that each party had different ideas about what they agreed to. These ambiguous, "fuzzy" agreements suffer from two sets of problems.

First, fuzzy agreements can be ambiguous because not all parties share the same understanding of *key words* that make up the agreement. It's hard to be accountable for something that isn't well defined. A good example is this common agreement: "We will respect each other." What does the word "respect" mean to you? To me, it includes many things, among them not interrupting me or talking over me. But to many people, interrupting is a perfectly acceptable way to converse and is in no way disrespectful. So these two different interpretations of what constitutes respect, which we believe we have agreed to, can actually lead to friction and resentment.

As you can probably imagine, this problem becomes more challenging when issues get more complex: What does "fiduciary responsibility to stakeholders" mean when a group is charged with deciding whether to expand operations and categories of "stakeholders" have differing interests?

When you clarify what you mean with key words and agreements, you are reinforcing your values and tying your actions into your inspiration.

The second problem of fuzzy agreements comes from lack of clarity about exactly *what is expected of the participants* in the agreement. We might agree that everyone is going to work on the year-end report. But if we have not made specific agreements about what each person will be accountable for, to whom, and by when, there is much room for differing interpretations and less than satisfying results.

Strong agreements require thoughtfulness and intention. It's all too easy to react in a situation and decide to act but not take the time to consider the bigger picture and possible implications. Such an incident occurred in an organization I was working with to help resolve tension between their general manager and the board of directors. The following situation was described to me.

Leave Me Out of This! (… but Wait!)

There was a lengthy discussion going on via email to brainstorm ideas for how to attract new members and donors to this nonprofit. The GM decided to opt out the emails, explaining that her workload was such that she didn't feel she had time to follow the debate and respond to every idea. She found the discussion burdensome and stressful at a time when she was facing other deadlines.

The board continued to discuss the issue over the next few weeks and came up with a plan, then brought it to the GM to implement. Her response? Anger! They had made a decision without consulting her! And she thought the plan they had come up with added impossibly to her workload. Many more hours were spent arguing about what might be a more realistic solution, and much effort was invested in resolving the anger and frustration that everyone felt.

The problem in this case was that when the GM bowed out of the email discussion, there was no explicit agreement about how a decision on the issue would be made. When she opted out, did that mean she was willing to accept whatever decision the board reached? Or did she expect to be brought back into the discussion at a particular point to review several options? Should the discussion have been put on hold until she could participate, or was there a more efficient way to weigh the options and come to a decision that wasn't so time consuming for everyone? Without a clear agreement about how they would arrive at a decision, the parties made different *assumptions* about what would happen. Tension and frustration were the result.

When you pause to consider the bigger picture and are more deliberate, you help everyone involved discover where explicit agreements can help you accomplish your goals efficiently and avoid conflict. The key is to focus on the outcome you are seeking. This will help you identify the points where more details are needed to make a strong agreement that will work.

This is not a common practice and can seem awkward at first. It may take more time to make agreements and decisions like this at the outset. But I think you will find that it is more effective and a better use of your time in the long run.

The bottom line is this: The ambiguity in fuzzy agreements means that they are left open to *personal assumptions and interpretations*. And that undermines the very potential of agreements.

Principle 3: Strong Agreements Leave No Room for Assumptions

Begin challenging your own assumptions. Your assumptions are your windows on the world. Scrub them off every once in a while, or the light won't come in.
—Alan Alda

As I said earlier, agreements by definition exist *between two or more people*. But when the agreement is not crystal clear, assumptions hold sway, and assumptions are a solo affair. They are *internal personal beliefs* that something is true or certain to happen even though we have no proof of that. It is the nature of assumptions that we act as though they're accurate even when they're not. To make matters worse, we also frequently act from the assumption that others share our assumptions when there is no evidence to suggest this is the case.

When assumptions and private interpretations get entangled in agreements, the potential for conflict is huge. Essentially, what this means is that *we are acting as though we have agreement* when in fact we don't. When we build expectations around assumptions in this fashion, we create the potential for misunderstanding at the least and failure at the worst.

We all know from experience that this is where most breakdowns in communication and understanding come from. Think of the last time you sent an email or left a phone message for a coworker asking for critical information on a project you are working on, assuming they would get back to you that day—or maybe the next—but by the fourth day you haven't heard from her. By then you're irritated and put out because her lack of response has held up your progress.

Even though we've all had to contend with the fallout of misunderstandings such as this, for the most part, we still haven't become skilled in testing our assumptions and making our agreements explicit, such as including along with our request for information a date and time by which we need someone's work. Better still would be to have a group discussion about how to communicate such requests so that everyone agrees on how to handle them—and that it is important *to* handle them, not just let them slide and create fertile ground for negative judgments and resentments.

Why We Make Assumptions

All of us have been advised at some time or another to be careful about making assumptions. We know they're the source of much trouble when they don't match what others think. So why is it so hard to get rid of them?

Assumptions are tricky because they have positive and negative value. On the one hand, they make it possible to function without constantly second-guessing ourselves and having to negotiate the rules for every moment. Each time we so much as engage in conversation, we operate from deep assumptions that everyone knows how to proceed and how to interpret what is being said. On the other hand, the same assumptions that facilitate cooperation can create serious problems of misunderstanding. Developing our awareness of assumptions and reevaluating them when needed can solve many problems.

The difficulty with assumptions is that it's challenging to bring into awareness things that we're not conscious of. Yet it is developing that skill that will eliminate many of the barriers to good communication and release more of the potential in groups. The section on Practices for Powerful Agreements at the end of this chapter will give you some guidance about how to make this easier. And structure helps, as we see in the next principle.

Principle 4: Strong Agreements Have Structure That Supports Accountability

Strong agreements address what, who, to whom, when, how, and "so what?" If any of these elements are missing, you have the potential for misunderstanding or lack of accountability. Let's continue with the simple example of meeting times to explore each of these components and how they set the foundation for accountability.

- *What outcomes* are we agreeing to be accountable for?
Example agreement: Staff meetings will be at 9 a.m. on Wednesday mornings.
Intended outcome: efficient meetings that accomplish the agenda.
- *Who* is accountable and *to whom?*
Example: We all are accountable *to each other* to be here and ready to start on time. Helen will be accountable to the group for actually starting the meeting at 9 a.m. sharp.
- *When* will the action take place?
Example: Each Wednesday at 9 a.m.
- *How* will we measure accountability?
Accountability for results is usually tracked in metrics. Accountability for conduct occurs as feedback.
Example: Joseph will keep a record of meeting times and attendance (metrics). The group will review that report quarterly (feedback).
- *So what* (if anything) happens if the agreement isn't kept?
What are the consequences for fulfilling or not fulfilling the agreement?
Example: Anyone who is late will pay $5 into the annual party kitty.

A note on consequences: There doesn't have to be any consequence for breaking an agreement beyond an honest acknowledgment that it's been broken; this will ensure that the group understands that it is taken seriously. Or, you can choose to have a "fun" consequence such as having to pony up for a party. If an agreement is critical, the consequence of breaking it might be more serious. The crucial point here is that there must be an honest accounting—in some form—of the success or failure of the agreement. The clearer the consequences are when the agreement is put in place, the more effective the agreement can be. Further discussion of consequences follows in Practices for Powerful Agreements below.

Principle 5: Strong Agreements Are Mutual

An agreement cannot be the result of an imposition.
—Nestor Kirchner

For an agreement to be powerful, it has to be intentionally joined by all parties involved. But this is not to say that all agreements have to be jointly designed or formed by consensus. Agreements can be formed in different ways and still be mutual.

Agreements by Acceptance

Some agreements are based on the requirements of one party, then accepted by another party. Employment contracts or codes of conduct are examples of this kind of agreement. Another example would be the contract for becoming a director of a nonprofit board. In these cases, the specifics of the agreement have been decided before the individual taking the job appears on the scene. Such agreements are often not negotiable: in order to work here you must agree to and abide by this set of rules. Even so, the agreement process supports a collaborative culture and accountability when it is consciously engaged by all of the parties involved.

> **"I'm Just Here for the Bennies"**
> This is illustrated by a story Mark Laret, the UCSF Medical Center executive we met in the chapter on inspiration, once told me. In the early days after he took over the job of turning the medical center back into a profitable and optimistic place to work, he was meeting with a group of staff people from across hospital departments. He asked why they worked there. As he went around the room, one woman said quite frankly that she worked there for the benefits. He matter-of-factly told her that if that was the case, there was no doubt another hospital that would be a better place to work. He was letting everyone know that joining the agreement about the direction the hospital was going in was nonnegotiable. But he also was acknowledging that it was a matter of her choice—it cannot be forced.

Agreements by Negotiation

Most agreements are reached through negotiation, whether formal or informal. This can be done between two individuals—we can agree to which part of the project we will each execute—or within the group, such as the ground rules that will be used for meetings.

Note to Leaders

When you embrace this practice of conscious agreements, you seize a great opportunity for raising the level of responsibility and accountability in your group. The model you provide by asking questions about agreements and taking responsibility for what you are agreeing to will elicit that same behavior from others. I realize this may require new skills for many leaders who are used to calling the shots; you will need to learn how to get clear about what agreements you need as a leader and be willing to make requests for those. The payoff in commitment and collaboration will be huge.

Whenever possible, the best decisions and agreements are reached through *consensus*. Consensus simply means reaching a decision that each person can commit to even if they didn't get exactly what they wanted. It can take some time to discuss all the considerations, but the decisions (agreements) reached in this way have full commitment of all the parties.

Consensus agreements are ideal because they do not allow for holdouts. When a decision/agreement is handed down from on high, it's always possible that some people don't agree with it so are not fully committed. The same is true when voting. It's easy to say, "Well, I voted against it, but they won, so good luck to them." A strong agreement doesn't arise simply as a result of majority rule or authority rule. This is where accountability often breaks down—where there is believed to be agreement but such a commitment was not actually achieved, or where someone is forced to go along even though they don't agree.

Learning to navigate the range of ways you can make agreements is important for achieving the kind of success that groups are truly capable of. Poor experiences, as well as misunderstandings about consensus or discussion-based modes of decision making, often keep people from developing the kinds of agreements and decisions that can fuel tremendous collective action. It is wise to explore different methods to find those that suit your purpose best.

Mixing It Up

One small business client of mine has found that a hybrid approach works extraordinarily well for his medical practice. After he identified the particular things that he felt were essential to require of his employees, he created contracts with each one that they agreed to by acceptance. But he has also increasingly found ways to bring everyone into decisions he used to make independently, such as whom to hire (after all, present employees have to help the new person be successful) and important procedural and office systems matters that help keep his medical practice running smoothly. He feels less stressed and everyone feels part of the team. They enjoy going to work! And their patients feel that.

Practices for Powerful Agreements

Now it's time to learn the tools for putting in place an agreements practice for your group. This is centered around making conscious, explicit agreements that align with and support your inspiration commitments.

Review Your Inspiration

Every group's foundational agreements are the defining stories it has adopted. All other agreements spring from them. Review your inspiration element: is everyone fully committed to your vision, mission, and goals? The willingness to make and keep agreements is based in the shared resolve you create in your inspiration practice. Check these basics, and then you can consider what agreements you need to make sure that you can achieve your aims.

Assess Your Agreements

There are five steps to assessing agreements. (To help with this you can download my Agreements Assessment Worksheet at www.groupalchemy.net/agree.)

1. Identify agreements that appear to be working and confirm that they are sufficient. Providing the opportunity for everyone in your group to evaluate your agreements is important in this step. There may be concerns you don't know about, or ideas for improvement that you can use. The method here might be as simple as a quick periodic check-in.

2. Identify the gaps. Where is the lack of an agreement causing unnecessary difficulty? *Tip:* Look for areas of discomfort to show you where agreements might be needed. Breakdowns in communication (such as the executive team in which some people felt they couldn't get a word in), points of friction, or places where things just don't seem to be working well are indications that work on agreements is needed.

   Often, the fact that expectations are not being met reveals where agreements are needed. For example, not long ago I was working with a consultant who did not meet a deadline we had set. When she also failed to notify me she'd be late and make a new agreement before the deadline arrived, I was frustrated and disappointed. That was when I realized that we needed another explicit agreement: what to do if a deadline was not going to be met.

3. Identify agreements that aren't working. What is preventing them from working? Does the agreement not fit the situation or is it the situation itself that needs to be changed? Is it a problem of fuzzy agreements that don't have the compo-

Informal Leadership
Remember that in the introduction to this book I emphasized that every member of the group can increase its success. Calling attention to hidden agreements that impede success and making requests for agreements that will instead support it are invaluable ways for each member to do just that.

nents of strong ones? What do you need to clarify? Make sure you agree on terminology and that everyone knows what is expected of them.

Again, breakdowns and conflict will point the way to areas where agreements are not sufficiently developed.

4.   Identify implicit agreements and determine whether or not they're working for you. It should be clear by now that the problem with implicit agreements is that they may not serve the interests of the group or the needs of its members. If you recognize this, you can proceed to identify them, assess their impact on the group's effectiveness, and create explicit agreements in their place that work.

Does it help or hinder the effectiveness of the group to have people checking their email during meetings? Would it be helpful to implement a practice whereby people share early stages of their work in order to get input and feedback? Are people having a hard time with the flow of discussion in meetings when multiple people are talking at the same time?

The answers to questions such as these are important to discover, but even more important is that *the group becomes conscious of the implicit agreements and assumptions it's been operating with, that it evaluates them, and that it consciously decides whether or not they serve the group's success.* Only then can it create the explicit agreements that will support its ambitions.

In the example of meeting start times, you can ask: Is it best to wait until certain people get to the meeting to begin? Does it help to have a flexible arrival time? If so, then talk about that and make an explicit agreement to that effect. Or does the implicit agreement lead to wasted time, frustration, cynicism, and later and later start times as people trickle in to avoid sitting and waiting? If so, then talk about that and make a meaningful agreement about how you start your meetings.

5.   Identify any assumptions that might be in the way of creating strong agreements. When you begin to discuss an issue, probe into the assumptions behind each point of view. Are new hires assuming that the most efficient course is best, without understanding regulatory requirements that unavoidably slow things down? Is long-time staff assuming that the way things are presently being done is the only option?

Following are a few more agreement assessment questions:

- Does your group have an agreement to make and keep agreements? Do you have an agreement to revise agreements as needed?

- Do you have ways to identify any agreements operating in the group that hinder your success?

- Does everyone in your group make requests when they need to resolve a problem or create a more productive environment?

- Do you work with discussion ground rules so that your meetings are productive and energizing?

- Do you leave meetings confident that everyone shares the same understanding of decisions reached and that everyone is completely committed to upholding them?

Make Strong Agreements

In light of your assessment and with your inspiration firmly in mind, you can negotiate agreements where you need them. Here's how:

1. Establish three foundational agreements and discuss what they mean to you:
    a. We agree to make and keep agreements.
    b. We agree to repair breakdowns.
    c. We agree to review agreements upon request and renegotiate when needed.

2. Create agreements that address both your structural arrangements, such as those concerning duties and roles, and agreements about conduct, such as during meetings. You can use the worksheet from your assessment to guide this process and make sure you have covered all of the bases.

    I recommend adopting the powerful ground rules that Roger Schwarz describes in his book *The Skilled Facilitator*. These will help you structure your discussions in the most productive and mutually respectful way possible. You might also find Stewart Levine's *The Book of Agreement* helpful. He provides wonderful guidance on a variety of different types of agreements.

3. Make sure your agreements explicitly address the structural components of strong agreements:

    What outcomes are we agreeing to be accountable for?

Who is accountable and *to whom?*
When will the action take place?
How will we measure accountability?
So what (if anything) happens if the agreement isn't kept?

4. Record important agreements so you have a basis for accountability.

"So What": Consider the Consequences

What happens if the commitment is not kept? This question poses serious issues for the effectiveness of the group so it is best addressed at the time the agreement is made. Without going into a punishment mentality, we need to consider how our handling of breakdowns affects the alchemy of the group. When the matter of consequences is not explicitly part of the agreement, there are several potential problems, falling into two categories.

If there is no prior agreement as to consequences, they can be handled arbitrarily.

This means that what happens after a breakdown can be based on personality, bias, mood, or whim, usually of the boss. Ever watch a boss treat different people differently on the same issue? One person gets reprimanded for being late and another gets away with it, for instance. When others in the group see that, it becomes a serious source of disenchantment and resentment that undermines the sense of ownership and commitment to the group. This is true for small matters such as being late. It is even more destructive in larger matters such as poor-quality work being accepted or excused.

People are reluctant to call others back to their agreements because they don't know what it means to do so.

Uncertainty about what might happen if the problem is raised can make people wary of bringing it up. This is especially true in the area of conduct and is exacerbated by the fact that most groups don't have agreements for what is acceptable conduct and how to handle unacceptable behavior. Managers are then left with the burden of figuring out what appropriate consequences are, and the midst of a breakdown is not usually the best time to make such decisions. Uncertainty can lead to inaction.

A stipulation of consequences in the agreement gives all parties an opportunity to *agree* to them, which has wonderful repercussions. It removes the blame and punishment quality that is so often confused with accountability. It also takes the pressure off the person or persons who have to deal with the outcome and decide whether consequences are necessary. While this will not be possible in all cases—or even necessary for most of the small agreements that occur in groups—where it is possible, it should be done.

Handle Breakdowns

When agreements are broken, those breakdowns need to be addressed so that integrity can be repaired. This is how you can avoid the problems of hidden agreements taking over we discussed earlier. Discuss how to handle breakdowns in agreements and how to request new agreements (see below). Consider making agreements about how to clean up if you mess up. What do you want to ask of each other regarding promptly addressing a problem you have created if you failed to meet an agreement? How do you go about taking the initiative to repair the breakdown if you notice it before someone else does? Do you want a protocol for getting assistance if people can't resolve the issue between themselves?

It might be worth practicing this in a nonthreatening situation, using role-play, for instance. It may take some time to reduce defensiveness and avoidance since many of us have not had a lot of experience with this kind of responsibility. The discussion in the next chapter on accountability and how to eliminate blame and shame will help with this issue.

Practice Making Requests for Agreements

Creating the explicit agreements you need to keep the group working optimally depends on *anyone* making a request for an agreement whenever she or he sees a need for one.

A source of ongoing frustration and resentment is situations where people don't feel at liberty to ask for what they see as necessary to eliminate a problem or a source of friction. This is why the practice of agreements includes making a group agreement to "make and keep agreements." That kind of primary agreement creates an explicit permission—and responsibility—to make requests when needed. This doesn't mean that every request results in the person who makes it getting their way. It's for the group to decide what is needed and appropriate; it's up to the individual to raise the issue so the group has the opportunity to address it. Two things will help with this.

- Get clear about the difference between complaining and making requests. This may take some practice because many of us are not accustomed to making requests and forming explicit agreements, especially when they concern personal behavior. If there is a strong habit of complaining and avoidance in your group, it is especially important to practice. Role-play can help bring humor and insight to this crucial habit. You might enact someone behaving badly during a meeting and let someone else make a request for a change in that behavior. Providing a concrete experience of making a request for an agreement about a difficult behavior helps develop customs in the group for how to handle these situations. This is what we did in the following example from one group I worked with.

"I Need a Hand!"

Two people in the facilities department were frustrated that no one offered help when they were carrying heavy boxes and equipment around the office. They expressed it as a complaint that included resentment as well as judgment about how unhelpful others in the group were. Upon hearing this, the rest of the group said they hadn't noticed they needed help; besides, in their minds, the facilities crew was so efficient and on top of things that there was no reason to think they didn't have it covered. I asked the facilities staff whether they had made any requests for help. They said no, that they didn't like to have to ask for help. It only took a few minutes to clarify their request and reach an agreement in the group; the heavy lifting was shared.

- Ground your requests in your inspiration. While personal needs are valid, this is not a license to satisfy personal whims or manipulate others to get our way. Requests for agreements need to be in service to the shared commitment.

   Pause and think about what your purpose is, as an individual and as a member of the group. Consider the situation at hand and what would help move your mission forward. Hold that uppermost in your mind when you think about and make your request.

   If you get a lot of push-back to your request, consider whether your perception of the situation is off base. Or do you need to explain your point of view better? Stay flexible.

Create a Structure for Your Agreement Practice

Make a commitment to routinely take some time to review your agreements and revise them as needed. Explore any communication breakdowns for areas where new agreements are needed, and create them. Put this on your calendar and make an *unbreakable* commitment to do it. The process might be as simple as taking five minutes at the end of a regularly scheduled meeting to assess. Or it might be a thirty-minute session during a review process. It is also good now and then to make a more substantial review.

While you can and should address agreement gaps and breakdowns in real time, as they happen, it's also important to have a time to discuss this area as a group when there are no deadlines or frustrations in the mix. A relaxed time gives people the opportunity to talk honestly about what's working, what's not, and what the group needs. Also, knowing that there is a regular time to do this can take the charge out of any day-to-day breakdowns that arise.

Remember, it's in our nature to make assumptions and fall into implicit agreements, so this work is never done. It is imperative to stay vigilant. I'll discuss this further in chapter 5 on the renewal element.

Agreements: Lessons Learned

Big success requires strong agreements.

Agreements shape and even determine much of our behavior. Yet many of the agreements we abide by go unnoticed and assumed. This means it's likely that you're working from implicit agreements that you have not yet recognized. Do all the agreements in your group live up to what you say you are committed to in your defining stories?

Many hidden agreements interfere with effectiveness. If we become more aware of these shadow agreements, discuss them, and make strong explicit agreements that work, we tap into the real power of groups.

Agreements are not straitjackets; they can always be renegotiated if this is done openly and with intention. The resistance some people have to engaging agreements powerfully may be a fear of being constrained. Having a strong agreement practice will help resolve that problem. If resistance is because of a desire to use ambiguity to maintain unilateral control or manipulate the situation, then a strong group agreement practice will help to expose that as well.

Simply making a commitment to develop strong agreements begins to change the nature of the environment you are operating in. Where there were uncertainty, confusion, judgment, and resentment, now there is room to test, question, voice confusion, and raise objections to what's going on because you have a stated willingness to take these group functions seriously. You can develop a new language and set of habits for addressing any situation that arises.

Strong Agreements Empower Accountability

With a powerful practice in agreements, the foundation is set for powerful accountability, the subject of the next chapter.

Resources

The Book of Agreement: 10 Essential Elements for Getting the Results You Want, Stewart Levine, Berrett-Kohler Publishers, 2002.

Conscious Business: How to Build Value Through Values, Fred Kofman, Sounds True Publishers, 2006.

The Four Conversations: Daily Communication That Gets Results, Jeffrey Ford and Laurie Ford, Berrett-Koehler Publishers, 2009.

The Skilled Facilitator, Roger Schwarz, Jossey-Bass, 2002.

Element Three:

Accountability

Cultivate confidence and trust

Build a culture of learning

Make better decisions

The key to growth is to make promises and to keep them.
—Stephen R. Covey

We have established now that agreements provide the structure for how people work together. But they only work when people have confidence in them and are assured that everyone in the group will do what they agree to. Agreements don't mean anything without accountability.

It's a truism that we need accountability in order to be successful; high performance cannot occur without it. We frequently hear a clarion call for "more accountability." Pick up a book on leadership or management and you will see plenty of ink spilled over questions of how to achieve it.

While there is no question that accountability is an essential element of success, it is often elusive. I think this is because it is generally entangled with a lot of concepts and attitudes that muddle what accountability really is and how it works. It gets conflated with responsibility and integrity, and it gets confused with blame and criticism. Then it gets handled in punitive ways that make it scary.

In the discussion that follows, we will look at how accountability can be detached from blame and criticism, how it is grounded in responsibility and motivated by inspiration, and how to establish the practices that will enable your group to encourage the integrity and reliability that lie at the heart of accountability. You will learn the practices that generate the genuine accountability that feeds extraordinary results. When you view accountability in the context of the culture of group alchemy, I think you will discover that it is readily attainable.

The accountability task of powerful groups is to create a feedback process that fosters learning and improvement.

Keeping Agreements

Accountability is simply an agreement to answer or "to account" for our actions. When we agree to be accountable, we are declaring a commitment: "You can count on me for x."

Like all agreements, then, it exists *in the relationship*. As Henry Evans says in his book *Winning with Accountability*, "It is not good enough to fulfill the commitment in our

Accountability Promotes Adaptation

All living things, including humans and our social groups, have to answer for their actions. Consider that organisms must adapt to their surroundings or face extinction. Societies also respond to their environments through what we call adaptive strategies, and the same is true for organizations. Survival and achieving the impact we seek are predicated upon getting accurate information from the environment about the effects of our actions. Accountability is a central piece of that process.

eyes—we have to fulfill the commitment in the eyes of others."

We can be accountable to ourselves, and in fact must be if we are going to be truly accountable to others. But our focus here is the accountability that exists *between people*—the reporting that satisfies others that we have done what we said we would do. This is what generates the trust and confidence in each other that create efficiency and effectiveness. Everyone can focus on their particular tasks because they can depend on others to do theirs as well. Decisions are reached more easily because everyone trusts one another to implement them.

Once you have a true accounting of the actions that members of your group have taken, you can make an accurate assessment of the efficacy of those actions; *accountability produces important information about what works.* This feedback loop of accounting and assessment is at the core of organizational learning and is essential to being able to adapt to rapidly changing environments.

The two facets of accountability—accounting and assessing—are sources of trust and information, essential to maintaining a strong culture that is capable of generating the results your group has committed to. Accountability is what keeps your culture aligned with your vision, values, and mission—the things you have declared as the reasons you exist.

Culture is based on what actually happens, not on the results people say they desire. And in organizations, results are a product of the culture. In anthropology we talk about "ideal culture" versus "real culture" to refer to the discrepancy between what people say they'll do and what they *actually* do. This gap is quite common; we espouse one set of values and beliefs but act in a different way. For example, American society has a traditional value of marriage as a lifelong commitment, but most marriages now end in divorce; the *actual* culture is one of serial monogamy. Within organizations, a common example of ideal versus real culture is found in those that espouse teamwork while actually operating with practices focused on individual performance and achievement.

We humans are very adept at discerning such discrepancies and responding to what people actually *do*. And we choose our behavior accordingly: inconsistencies in accountability will encourage more of the same. If we are not holding each other accountable to what we agreed to, then standards, behavior, and results devolve to what people are able to get away with. Self-interest begins to prevail over group commitments.

Fortunately, our work in agreements has set the stage for true accountability. *What we are accountable for is what we have agreed to.* Recall that strong agreements are structured to provide for accountability because they are clear and specific—with accountability measures built into them.

When your members make an explicit foundational agreement to make and keep agreements, as I suggested in the last chapter, you are making an unequivocal commitment to accountability. And when you engage the practices for accountability you will find in this chapter, you make accountability both desirable and easy.

At the beginning of this chapter I mentioned that our ideas about accountability are often muddled, and this makes achieving it difficult. So before we dive into the benefits that will accrue to your group when good accountability practices are in place, let's take a moment to get clear on a very important distinction that will increase your understanding of this essential element of group alchemy.

Accountability and Responsibility Are Not the Same

To develop powerful accountability, you need to understand the distinction between accountability and responsibility and then develop conscious habits in each. People often use the terms interchangeably, and this is fuzzy thinking that creates a lot of confusion and denies us the power of each of these important behaviors of success. Each has a different origin and associated practices, and when they're conflated people don't know how to work effectively with either one.

Whereas accountability exists in relationship and is *external* to the individual, it comes from an *internal state of mind* we call responsibility. This is why I have named accountability rather than responsibility an element of *group* alchemy. Another way to say this is that accountability is the manifestation of the internal state of mind that we call responsibility *as expressed in the relationship to the group.*

The core meaning of the word responsibility is simply the *ability to respond.* When we choose to exercise that ability, it's because we have a sense of *ownership* of the situation at hand. Recognizing the ability to respond as the essence of responsibility is the heart of a powerful but uncommon perspective that opens tremendous potential for extraordinary success. Christopher Avery's applied research with leaders reveals the mind's Responsibility Process, which is a valuable resource for developing this approach. I draw on his work here.

In a group that has shared commitments and rewards, *everyone* in the group is equally responsible for its success. This, simply yet profoundly, means that we all have the ability to respond to situations and can take actions that will contribute to the group's goals and objectives. We are all responsible for our organization's mission. Avery clarifies what this means when he says, "This kind of complete ownership of what happens does not mean we are responsible for another person. It is not to say, 'I caused this' but is about responding for the cause."

This is why strong inspiration practices are important. It is from a sense of *responsibility* for the mission, goals, and overall success of the group that each member signs on to specific tasks and outcomes.

By contrast, you are *accountable* for the specific tasks and outcomes that your job requires of you. You might be accountable for financial systems while someone else is accountable for human resources development and another person for janitorial services. You all are responsible for advancing the group's defining stories even though each of your responses is different.

When we share the group inspiration and are moved to take responsibility, we will serve the group even beyond the narrow scope of duties for which we are strictly accountable. We will do whatever we can to address the needs of the group and help it reach its goals. There is no sitting back and watching while someone else struggles or flounders because it's "not my concern." The effectiveness of the group and of the whole enterprise *is* my concern.

I saw this happen on a grand scale with one client that faced a crisis.

It's Not My Job—And I'm Responsible

The financial department of a large hospital made a substantial error in the billing system that resulted in underbilling for a whole class of procedures. The problem went undiscovered for almost a year. By the time it came to light, the shortfall amounted to multiple millions of dollars and thrust the company into a financial crisis—precisely at the time when battles over health care reform had introduced a great deal of uncertainty into the system. Almost overnight, the company went from a cash-healthy, expanding organization to a contracting organization fighting for its very survival.

When I met with the executive team shortly after the charging error was discovered, they were still in shock, but they chose to accept their responsibility and take action.

Acknowledging his position as CFO, James declared that he was accountable for the financial health of the company and he owned that he was accountable for the error. While none of the other executives had that specific accountability, they all recognized that they each had responsibility for the health and success of the hospital and responded to the crisis by taking that responsibility seriously. They moved on from the loss and each rallied to identify what she or he could do in each of their areas to address the problem and bring the company back to financial health. They took big hits to their division budgets, redesigned some of their management systems, and took concerted action to work together more effectively as a team. What didn't occur? Blaming or "not my job" statements. This was the responsibility aspect of accountability in action.

Now that you have a foundation in the important distinction between responsibility and accountability, let's have a look at what healthy accountability practices can do for your group. (Later, in Principles of Accountability, we will look at some of the other concepts that can become conflated with accountability, such as criticism and blame.)

The Alchemy of Accountability

Accountability begins with a declaration of commitment—what you can count on me for in the future. By making this declaration about the future, we *create a present* that fosters helpful qualities. Here are some of the qualities this cultivates in the group.

Initiative and Ingenuity

Good accountability practices build an environment of certainty and optimism. People can move forward with confidence when they know what they are accountable for and what they can count on others for. They are also free to be creative and take initiative if they know they won't be punished or blamed if things don't work out as the group hoped they would.

Ongoing Inspiration

When accountability is practiced consistently, the responsibility people feel for the mission is validated. The diligent practice of inspiration is reinforced and supported.

Confidence and Trust

Genuine accountability creates the confidence and trust that enable people to take decisive action and remain inspired. Trust is born out of our experiences of group members doing what they say they will do. When the group holds a high standard of accountability and practices full responsibility, we are assured that our efforts aren't wasted. We know that we can count on each other and we don't have to second guess each other.

Learning, Quality Decision Making, and Improvement

Accountability is fundamentally about learning. Getting an accurate accounting of what has happened gives us valuable information. We learn what works and what doesn't and we can make any necessary course corrections. Decisions are informed by accurate, high-quality information.

For example, let's say I'm accountable for running my program on budget. When I let the group know that it's going over budget, we have information: either we are not operating as we should or we misjudged what it would take to run the program. We can conduct further analysis (accounting) and decide what adjustments (corrections) need to be made. We either need to change something in our operations or we need to change our expectations and the budget, and we can examine this choice together.

In this light, accountability is seen as intrinsically beneficial, as the way we learn and develop in order to accomplish more of what we want. This includes the results we want to see in the world as well as positive relationships in the group.

Two things become possible when we hold ourselves accountable and ask others to do the same. Both lead to success. Either the accounting step of accountability reveals that you have succeeded—in which case there is reason to celebrate and you know specifically what worked and how—or the accounting reveals that you have missed the mark. In that case you get information about what you can do to correct your course. This, too, is inspiring. In both cases, you are learning and that's where the power for success exists. You do better problem solving and make better decisions.

People Feel a Sense of Ownership and Take Responsibility for the Group and Its Success

When you are accountable to others, you inspire them to be the same. The reverse is also true; as you see others being accountable, you are motivated to be accountable yourself. A sense of ownership for the group's success is reinforced throughout, evident in the ways people take responsibility. You find that members *seek* ways to take action above and beyond their assigned duties for the sake of the results the group has committed to. This is expressed in the team member who volunteers to stay late and help a coworker finish a project even though she isn't assigned to it. Or the person who brings in a well-thought-out proposal for revising a program to increase efficiency without being asked to do so.

People Are Not Distracted by "Difficult Personalities"

The domineering or obstructive personalities that people often complain about in groups, including bullies, cannot dominate when you hold everyone accountable to what you have all agreed is the best way to go about achieving your mission.

The problem of "difficult personalities" and their effect on group effectiveness is the subject of countless books and workshops; it is obviously a serious and perennial problem. Following the group alchemy formula means that the group has the power to refuse to let disruptive behavior impede or detract from its efforts. If practicing true accountability doesn't solve the problem, it will be clear to all when a disruptive person needs to leave the group.

It's important to take these problems very seriously; they are clearly a drag on the success of the group and can be very personally painful, even damaging in the case of bullying. I have seen too many groups that don't take injurious behaviors seriously enough and end up significantly compromising their success and their members' well-being.

One study by Will Felps, Terrence Mitchell, and Eliza Byington reported loss of performance of *30 to 40 percent* when there was just one of what they call "bad apples" in a group. (They use names for the bad applies such as "jerk" for someone who violates norms of respect, or "deadbeat" for one who slacks off, or a "downer" who is always pessimistic.) These researchers recommend getting rid of the rotten fruit. I agree that in some cases this may be absolutely necessary but I think it is wise to practice group alchemy and the accountability process first. It might be possible to encourage more productive behavior from the offending person, and—most importantly—while attempting to do so you will strengthen your culture and *reinforce the positive conduct of everyone else in the group.* When you use the agreement practices in the preceding chapter and the accountability practices I outline further in this one, your group will have the prerequisite agreements that counterproductive behavior will not be tolerated *and* you will have a language for addressing transgressions of those agreements.

The very reason those bad apples can have the detrimental effect they do is that they aren't being held accountable for their actions. And even though a few individuals may prove irredeemable, most groups experience some degree of negative behaviors at various times from people who have great talents to contribute to the cause. (Many of us, in fact, even with best intentions, could occasionally be guilty of such behaviors.) It's not always a simple question of purging the rotten apples.

Interrelated Elements
The topic of accountability provides an opportunity to emphasize the interrelated impacts of each element of group alchemy. Sometimes the problem of "personality" boils down to people not having fully committed to clear shared *inspiration.* Or it comes from a lack of conscious, explicit *agreements* that everyone has signed on to, so there is no basis upon which to hold people accountable for their impact on the group. You can see how these elements of the group alchemy formula build on each other to create a culture that supports success.

Attracting People, Resources, and Partners

People of integrity who have skills and resources to contribute and who practice accountability and responsibility naturally migrate to people and organizations that share these qualities. And they run far and fast from those that don't.

Radical Accountability

A dramatic case in point comes from the international development organization Water For People. They have opted for a fairly radical level of transparency and accountability. They post real results—they call them report cards—from their project to provide safe water to people around the world on their website (www. waterforpeople.org). They don't just present the information that makes them look good; they present what is actually happening and the level of impact they're having. When asked by a journalist whether this level of honesty was risky when it came to attracting donors, their director said that he sees it actually improving relations with donors. It inspires their trust, "bypasses skepticism" about their success claims, *and* has opened up *more* room for assistance, ideas, and partnerships to turn their failures into successes. All indications are that full accountability is improving their results.

The Cost When Accountability Is Weak

Confusion over accountability and its associated internal aspect, responsibility, generates two kinds of problems: people don't take responsibility and they are not held accountable. Each is debilitating in its own way, and sometimes they occur together. Because this can be so problematic, and because I'm frequently asked to help solve these problems, I want to take time to describe how they have manifested in groups I have worked with.

People Don't Take Responsibility

A typical notion of responsibility is that I am not responsible for outcomes I'm not explicitly accountable for. This is the "It's not my job" problem. An example of this occurred in one organization I worked with.

Not Me—I Don't Like To!

A nonprofit drug and alcohol treatment and rehabilitation organization in Northern California was losing state and county grant funding that accounted for 60 percent of its budget. It had two choices: find new ways to raise the money or drastically cut its programs. As it happened, this organization was the only resource for such programs in the entire county. During a strategy meeting the directors were discussing ways the board could raise money. One of the members spoke up emphatically in response and said, "I didn't join the board to raise money. I don't know anything about it and I don't like it. I'm not going to start asking for money."

This example of turning your back on a serious problem and saying, "You fix it!" results from not understanding the nature of responsibility. You stepped into responsibility for the group when you accepted the job (whether volunteer or paid); you took responsibility for that organization's success. Unfortunately, this is not widely recognized or practiced and the lack of doing so is the source of much mediocrity. In fact, we can use our very narrow notion of responsibility as a way to avoid accepting that larger level of it. "I can't be responsible. I don't know anything about fundraising . . ." rather than saying, "Let's see what I can learn about fundraising so I can make a difference here."

The "It's not my job" problem is exacerbated by the notion that if I'm not in charge, I can't be responsible. Unless I've accepted responsibility for a specific thing, it's for the boss to handle. The necessity to resolve this kind of dysfunction is why it's critical to have a group conversation and for all members to understand the distinct roles of responsibility and accountability.

No One Has Clear Accountability

It is all too common in my work that when I'm asked for help I immediately see that *no one in the group has accepted clear accountability* for an outcome or task that the group has deemed important. This is usually a by-product of sloppy practices. Discussions are held, opinions expressed, decisions reached, but no accountability structure is made explicit. People leave the discussion thinking that what they understand to be the conclusion is what everyone else understands as well. Here's an example.

An Expensive Assumption

The staff of a small nonprofit discussed the need for completing the program evaluation requirements for their foundation grant. There was a lengthy discussion about the different components of the reporting requirements and who would take care of them. The discussion bounced back and forth between the program director and the development director as to how best to handle this. Two months later when the director asked Sondra, the program director, about one of the reports, her response was "I thought we agreed that Reggie (the development director) was doing that." This was an expensive assumption. They failed to file the report on time and lost their chance to reapply for funding.

A One-Two Punch: No Responsibility or Accountability

When people are not practicing accountability *and* no one is taking responsibility, big messes result. I will use meetings as an example again because they commonly exhibit both of these weaknesses.

I cannot count the number of times I've heard people complain about their experience of meetings. They roll their eyes, sigh heavily, and shrug their shoulders. I recently heard a CEO say, "Unfortunately, this means another meeting." This is a serious problem because meetings are actually one of the *best* opportunities for the creative exchange of ideas, for re-experiencing the group's inspiration and connection, and for creating success. Still, I know this isn't common experience in most meetings. The reason is frequently a *combination* of failing to practice both responsibility and accountability. Here's a good example of the problem.

Oh, and About the Kids . . .

A teacher at a middle school described a faculty meeting to me in which forty-five minutes were spent on deciding on a centerpiece for an annual awards luncheon. Then five minutes were spent on the problem of kids not reading at the level they should. She was peeved at the foolishness of this disheartening misuse of time and told me it occurs regularly. She wasn't alone in her frustration either; many of the people in that meeting complained about it afterward.

The Missing Responsibility in This Scenario: The breakdown here occurred because no one chose to act on their responsibility to ensure a productive outcome for the meeting. Whether or not focusing on choosing a centerpiece was the best use of the faculty meeting time, the question was never asked so there was no opportunity to refocus the meeting. No one raised the issue with the group or asked for changes in how the meeting would be conducted. And no one volunteered to do anything to help improve the meeting, such as facilitate, serve as timekeeper, or make sure the group stuck to the meeting agenda.

The "I'm-not-in-charge-so-I'm-not responsible" notion was pervasive in this situation. People wondered why the principal, who was conducting the meeting, didn't rein it in. No one thought to take responsibility for it themselves.

The Missing Accountability: The other problem is that there was no mechanism for accountability in this meeting. In many such cases, *no one* is accountable for the quality of the meetings because there are no agreements about what a quality meeting looks like and who will see to it that the meeting fits that description. Clearly there was no formal and public accounting of whether the meeting was accomplishing what participants felt was important, let alone how people were conducting themselves. There was plenty of private accounting going on, though, in people's complaints to their friends when it was over!

Other Impacts of Weak Accountability

You will probably recognize some or all of these additional symptoms of missing accountability from your own experience of working in groups that don't live up to their potential.

Informal Leadership
Each member of the group can impact the way accountability is practiced in the group. It's not just a matter for those in a formal leadership position. The most powerful thing anyone can do is to develop these practices personally. Then you can ask for them from others. The change in group culture you would like to see begins with you.

When the group doesn't possess accountability and responsibility skills, people are left to defensive actions: *blaming, shaming, guilt, avoidance, denial, and withdrawal* are the results. Relationships deteriorate. People look out for themselves rather than the group. Cliques form. Bullies emerge. Hostility and resentment build.

Poor or erratic accountability means that we don't know what to expect. It's difficult to act with certainty in such a climate. *Group members lose trust and confidence.*

Cynicism and resignation set in. The fastest way to create cynicism in your group is to make agreements without holding anyone accountable for them. If we set goals but don't measure our results, our goals really don't mean anything. The question arises: why bother making agreements in the first place? They mean nothing without accountability; they're just hot air—a waste of time. If we don't mean it when we say we're going to do something, then why believe anything else we say? We have moved onto the slippery slope that drains the life energy from the group's purpose and inspiration.

Quality and results decline. Without accurate accounting, how do we know what really happened, what was effective, and what was not effective, so we can make the best decisions about what to do next? Accountability is a critical locus of information for the organization's learning. Without it, weak or false information is used to make decisions, solve problems, and set policies.

Not holding people accountable for a high standard of excellence creates a *culture of mediocrity*. It is not possible to sustain high quality over time in the face of inconsistent accountability.

The disappointment and frustration that follow from not being part of a successful venture means that responsible people leave. *The group loses talent.* Turnover becomes endemic.

Reflection Questions

1. Do your group's members show that they are willing to accept full responsibility for the consequences of the decisions and actions of the group as a whole?

2. Do you trust your colleagues to deliver on their commitments?

3. Are power plays and manipulation nonexistent (or at least rare)?

4. When things go wrong, do members look to solve the problem rather than avoid it, hide it, or simply find fault?

5. Do members of the group provide honest assessments of each other's work and contributions in the framework of your mission and goals?

6. If someone is not behaving in a manner consistent with your agreements, does someone else in the group raise that issue and call them back to your agreements?

Principles of Accountability Practice

While the basic meaning of accountability is simple—we all answer for our actions—a closer look reveals core principles that will help make accountability a significant source of success in your group. Whenever you're experiencing difficulty with accountability, you can be sure the problem lies with one or more of these principles. Let's explore each of these in turn.

Principle 1. Accountability Is Grounded in Inspiration and Agreements

Accountability is ultimately about our shared commitments. Taking responsibility for the group's success and holding yourself accountable to it can feel futile in an environment where people don't feel connected to the bigger picture. It's the vision of what you are creating together that provides motivation and context for accountability.

This, combined with the next principle that ties accountability to agreements, links accountability to the group and ensures that it is consistent, not arbitrary. Personal issues and arbitrary opinions are not involved. Accountability is not an opportunity to beat up on others or manipulate them to do what you want.

Principle 2. Accountability Depends on Strong, Explicit Agreements

Accountability cannot exist in the absence of strong agreements. When assumptions and expectations are left vague or implicit—if they're "fuzzy"—accountability is impossible. If you haven't begun with a conversation to create clear and explicit agreements and commitments, the necessary conditions to achieve accountability simply don't exist. This is the first place to look when accountability seems to be breaking down.

As we learned in the last chapter, agreements are a sure-fire antidote to assumptions. When we assume that someone else will be accountable in the way we *imagine* they will, we create the opportunity for disappointment. This problem can exist as a casually stated remark, such as "Let's get together on Friday afternoon to talk about this." Both parties say yes and go their separate ways, thinking that they have settled something. But there may be different levels of commitment to that meeting, with one person putting it on her calendar and another figuring he'll see how his Friday morning goes and then decide whether he can make it. Each party has decided to be accountable *to a different agreement*—a recipe for confusion at the least and anger and resentment at worst.

Assumptions can also be more substantive. A client recently told me, for example, about receiving a very poor performance review from her boss. She was understandably upset about it. He told her that she was too much of a perfectionist and as a result spent too much time on tasks he didn't think were important. The real problem, however, was a grievous lack of agreement; she had never even been given a job description, let alone clear guidelines for what high-quality performance would look like! She had been left to make it up on her own and then told she had fallen short of her boss's (unspoken) expectations. This situation did not support her personal commitment and growth.

In matters large and small, it's not hard to see how lack of explicit and clear agreements leads to misunderstandings and the belief that others are not acting accountably.

Principle 3: Accountability Applies to Both Results and Conduct

People are generally accustomed to thinking about accountability in terms of results. This is the common emphasis in our organizations and institutions, so this measurement of accountability is usually well developed. It often takes the form of an annual report, a program evaluation, or an annual employee review.

Equally important is accountability to the group's agreements and personal conduct in the group. This is true for two reasons. First, how people behave in the group is instrumental to its ability to achieve the intended results. Second, accountability for agreements about conduct in support of the group is critical to maintaining the group's overall integrity in agreements as well as its inspiration. In short, accountability for group behavior builds and strengthens the fabric of group alchemy that supports outstanding performance and results.

The conduct dimension of accountability involves addressing more personal situations than are typically found in the results dimension and thus can elicit more emotion.

This can be uncomfortable and challenging, so conduct is often not handled at all until there's a crisis. The story of the executives with different meeting styles in the previous chapter is a good example of this.

Many of us don't have a lot of positive experience addressing personal behavior. Most people don't want to be critical or mean and don't have a model for calling out mistakes or unproductive behavior in ways that are neither. And all of us fear disconnection: remember our human impulse to be connected in groups.

These feelings can make it very difficult to call people to account for behavior that we find objectionable or that we think hinders our success. But we have to keep in mind that we aren't doing anyone any favors if we don't address lapses in follow-through on agreements. Compassionate feedback about what works and what doesn't is critical to maintaining and improving upon what works.

The principles that follow, along with Practices for Accountability later in the chapter, help make this easier.

Principle 4. Accountability Happens in the Group

The kind of accountability that supports group alchemy happens in the group. It is not managed by a "person-in-charge." The fact is that accountability or the lack of it already exists in the group; it just may not be openly addressed as such.

Consider that each member's actions affect the other group members and the overall success of the group. They also may directly affect others' ability to meet their personal commitments. When people are committed to the group and its success—when they have all taken *responsibility* for the group—vertical accountability, managed by the boss, undermines that commitment.

In the group alchemy model, it's up to everyone to help each other keep their agreements, achieve results individually and collectively, and support the group's effectiveness. Powerful group results are a product of *mutual accountability*.

Being Accountable to the Group

The treasurer on a nonprofit board shared his frustrations with me. A board member who had agreed during a board meeting to produce a fundraising report had not done so. The treasurer was very concerned about the financial health of the organization and the need to get moving on an upcoming fundraising drive.

He asked me how he should handle the problem and whether he should go to the board president so she could follow up. After confirming that the board member had made the original commitment to produce the report with the whole group present and involved, I suggested to the treasurer that instead he bring it up at the next board meeting. In this way, accountability *to the group* would be reinforced and dealt with openly. The group would thus have the opportunity to act from its inspiration, acknowledge the impact on everyone in the group of this lapse in accountability, and have the opportunity to reinforce its identity—to once again answer the question: What kind of group are we?

> **Formal Leadership**
> As the formal group leader you have a special impact on the quality of accountability in your group. Are you acting with integrity yourself and supporting it in your group? This calls for flawless and irreproachable personal integrity and resisting the temptation to fall into the "Do as I say, not as I do" syndrome.

Of course, there are employment situations that involve accountability in a hierarchical line of authority, but it is best to minimize this as much as possible. The paternalistic nature of hierarchical organizations sends the message "I'm in charge; you're not," which undermines the sense of ownership that is at the heart of personal responsibility. The premise here is that *your success as a group will increase as you decrease the need for such vertical accounting.*

Indeed, there are many kinds of groups in which vertical accountability makes no sense. When there is no single person in charge, as is the case with nonprofit boards, university faculties, and other professional peer-level work groups, leadership and accountability are more widely dispersed throughout the group. It is partly as a result of my involvement in many such groups that I developed this group alchemy approach—I saw so many of them struggle to find multilateral modes of accountability, responsibility, and leadership.

When you have genuine group commitments, people are empowered to ask each other for accountability and not wait for someone "in charge" to enforce it. This allows everyone in the group to be "owners" of the group's success, and it takes a tremendous load off the group's leaders, who are freed to invest their energies in more powerful ways.

A Multilateral Accountability Story

A group I worked with had established clear agreements that included being on time for meetings, yet one member persisted in coming late. This particularly bothered one of his colleagues, who felt it showed disrespect to the rest of the group. She told me that *because they had an explicit agreement, made in the group* to be on time, she felt empowered to speak directly to this person about how it affected her, even though she was not the "person-in-charge." When she did so, he heard her *accounting* of his failure to uphold the agreement and told her he hadn't realized how much it mattered to her and others. He recommitted to coming to meetings on time, and did so from then on. "The boss" never had to get involved.

Principle 5. Accountability Depends on Integrity

Accountability has to be reliable. It demands consistency and impeccability, both important components of personal and group integrity. If accountability is applied in an arbitrary or uneven fashion, it means nothing and it falls apart. Even in a matter as seemingly small as what time a meeting starts, as we saw in the last chapter, your group creates and re-creates your standards for accountability. It is in such small matters that "slack" is introduced and allowed to become endemic, even customary.

Questions such as these develop: When does accountability matter and when does it not? What does a meeting start time say about accountability? Integrity can easily lapse when it's clear that no one truly values integrity enough to call for it. Stephen M. R. Covey eloquently points this out in his book *The Speed of Trust*. Small chips in the walls will eventually bring down a whole building.

Accountability is dependent upon the willingness to be honest and consistent in what we say and do. It goes without saying that dishonesty, deception, and manipulation are antithetical to accountability, but focusing on these shortcomings in others denies us the opportunity to build accountability. We cannot make someone else act with integrity. We can, however, create the conditions that encourage and reward it. We can decide that we will not accept less.

Integrity is made easier by strong practices in agreements and accountability. When you make the first agreement for any group—to make and keep clear agreements—you have agreed to be accountable and established the foundation for integrity. Any evidence that someone is not exercising integrity—matching actions to words—is addressed through the accountability process the group has agreed to. Because it occurs compassionately and in the context of your group inspiration, this does not take the form of a personal attack; instead it is an assessment about whether an action serves the group's mission. We'll look at the process for this further along in the section on practices for accountability.

Principle 6. The Focus Is on Learning, Not Criticism

With good accountability in place, people talk honestly about how things are going. They aren't afraid to call others to account if they see that a commitment has not been kept; that's because this is considered valuable feedback *for the sake of the cause*. This includes both domains of success: performance results and personal behavior in the group.

Barry Schwartz and Kenneth Sharpe speak eloquently about accountability as learning in their book *Practical Wisdom: The Right Way to Do the Right Thing*. They emphasize that it's through being honest and reflective about the mistakes you make that you can access the "practical wisdom" that comes from learning what went wrong and what you can do better. They acknowledge that this takes courage—particularly in environments that have not created an open learning environment. One example they use is that of hospital mortality-and-morbidity conferences. These are meetings doctors hold when someone dies under their care in order to discuss how mistakes that may have contributed to the death could be prevented in the future. Keeping these venues free from adverse consequences gives people the opportunity to talk openly and honestly about their mistakes and everyone can learn more and do better.

This kind of accountability isn't about giving criticism, "constructive" or otherwise. Criticism comes from a position of superiority and is based on disapproval. It generates defensiveness and is not an environment for learning.

I recently heard a woman in one of my workshops say that she used to have a hard time with criticism, but she taught herself how to handle it so that she could improve. I immediately admired this woman's determination and commitment to herself and her performance. At the same time, I was reminded of how important the context is for feedback so that it promotes learning, not defensiveness.

People get stuck in "constructive criticism" when they don't have the tool of powerful accountability. Attempting to make criticism sound palatable by calling it "constructive" actually says, "I am pretending to be nice but I really think you are wrong and I am right." Accountability, by contrast, is based on mutual learning: what can we figure out together about what will work best?

Tony Schwartz at The Energy Project encourages what he calls "deconstructive criticism." When you feel the need to criticize "constructively," don't assume that you're right. Be curious and open-minded rather than making declarations and coming to conclusions. In other words, be accountable for your own impressions and interpretations, and help maintain a learning environment.

Principle 7. Blame Has No Role in Accountability

Committing to accountability as learning separates it from blame. Blame will not serve your efforts to get powerful results.

We could argue that a particular individual is to blame for not filing a report or making a mistake in the billing structure, but stop and consider whether this contributes to the group and its success. Synonyms for blame are "indict," "condemn," "incriminate." It's rare that any such act can further the cause of getting good results.

The fact is that most people are doing the best they can. If you have someone in your group who isn't, you need to ask why you are carrying that person. But if you assume that people are doing their best, if what they're doing doesn't work or they make a mistake, they need to hear that and have the opportunity to improve.

When accountability is mixed with blame, it becomes a weapon for punishment and control. This may make sense in an extreme case such as an individual who has committed a capital crime, but in organizations the consequence of entangling blame with accountability is that when the word accountability comes up, people feel nervous or threatened. It takes on punitive and demoralizing qualities and contributes to avoidance, denial, and misrepresentation—the very opposite of accountability.

Blame and criticism tend to be the default when agreements and a shared commitment to accountability are missing. A strong agreement practice helps prevent this problem when paired with the accountability process we will turn our attention to next.

Practices for Powerful Accountability

You can't make other people be accountable or responsible, or force them to act with integrity, but you absolutely can create the conditions that call out and support those behaviors. And each of us individually can cultivate them within ourselves and call on them in those around us.

If you want greater accountability, you need to weave it into the fabric of your culture: to create context and structure for it so it becomes a habit. This, like every other element of group alchemy, requires a structure that supports consistent accountability practices. It is helpful to begin with review and assessment.

Real Culture
Recall the discussion in the beginning of this chapter about the problem of discrepancy between "ideal culture" and "real culture." For the purposes of creating a powerful culture in your group that is capable of leading you to great success, it's important for you to be very honest about what your "real culture" is so that you can bring your actions into alignment with your values. If you truly want to encourage and support excellence, denial or wishful thinking will not serve you in this.

Review (or Develop) the Foundation for Accountability: Your Inspiration

Review your inspiration and confirm that your vision and mission truly reflect the group's aspirations, and that individuals see their personal ambitions and aspirations in it. Are people genuinely committed to your inspiration?

Make sure your goals have accountability built into them. They must specify the intended results in ways that are measurable. And they must specify who is accountable and by when. Without these, all you have are wishes and dreams. See below for details on how to structure this.

Review (or Develop) the Framework for Accountability: Your Agreements

- *Make sure you have a specific agreement for how your group handles accountability.* This agreement forms the backbone of your accountability practice. An agreement that you *will* hold yourselves and each other accountable should include *how* you will handle accountability for both results and conduct. This requires an agreement to deal with breakdowns *in the group as they happen* rather than act as though they don't matter. This is where most groups falter.

- *Make sure each of your agreements has an accountability component.* Group alchemy means being explicit about accountability. This is why every agreement and decision you make needs to have clear accountability attached to it.

- Review the chapter on agreements, in particular the structure for strong agreements:

  What outcomes?

  Who and to whom?

  How?

  So What?

Conduct an Accountability Assessment

Powerful accountability begins with being accountable for *what is actually happening now* in your organization. Find out: where is accountability working and where are there gaps?

- Determine whether each agreement in your group has clear accountability associated with it.

- Are people being held accountable to these agreements in both the areas of results and personal conduct?

- Are some people more accountable than others?

- How do you know whether you are living up to your commitments? Do you have clear measures for accountability for each of these areas: performance goals, strategic goals, and agreements?

You can use a variety of measurement tools such as surveys, questionnaires, focus groups, or whole-group discussions, as appropriate to your situation. Linda Galindo's book *The 85% Solution* offers some valuable questionnaires that can help guide you in this process. Her work does a good job of addressing personal accountability in particular.

For instance, a survey will give you an overview of your situation. Then you might use a case study approach if a particular situation is especially important or complex and you need more in-depth information about where accountability has been lacking. This could help you deconstruct what took place and ensure that you get to all the critical factors that prevented accountability. Was a goal not met because resources were not made available? Or was it not met because conditions in the economy changed?

Agree To Use the Following Process for Handling Breakdowns in Agreements About Conduct

Breakdowns occur when actual events don't match what we said would happen. These must be resolved in a manner that supports ongoing group success. That means an accurate accounting of what happened followed by an appropriate response. Special attention may be needed to build the structure and skills for addressing breakdowns in the area of personal conduct because of the discomfort that often surrounds those situations, particularly at first. There are healthy, compassionate, constructive ways to address breakdowns, beginning with the context of group alchemy in which breakdowns are viewed as opportunities for learning and renewal. That promise is achieved through skillful handling of the situation. The following points will help you on that path.

- *Handle it now.*

  Whenever possible, accountability for conduct agreements is best handled in real time, when the breakdown occurs. This involves calling out the group's agreement and the individual behavior that is in contradiction to it. Remember that ignoring it or wishing it away can wreak havoc on your group and its potential.

- *Process the breakdown as a group.*

  Unless it's strictly a one-on-one situation, a breach in agreement should be processed in the group. Recall that anything less allows for disintegration of the group.

  If I have failed to follow through on a promise to the group or behaved in a way that has disrupted the group's ability to work effectively, I am accountable for that to everyone. I get to step into responsibility and own my behavior and ask, What can I do? The group can then decide how to fairly resolve the matter. This honors the commitment to the group.

- *Schedule periodic accountability check-ins.*

  Periodic check-ins can be helpful in addressing small matters or the gradual erosion of integrity that can happen in any group. Be preemptive and address what's really happening so that small disappointments do not become the status quo. Decide how you will do this: At the beginning of each meeting? Quarterly? During an annual review? For more ideas on this, see chapter 5 on renewal.

- *Look for indicators of breakdowns and discuss these in your group.*

  When I ask clients to describe their experience in groups that don't work well, they use words like *negativity, poor communication, arguments, criticism, frustration, sadness, depressed, resentful, shut down, lack of motivation, lack of trust, waste of time.* These are excellent indicators that breakdowns are happening. (They may also indicate the need to make agreements if there are none.) What words does your group use to describe breakdowns? Create your own list and watch for their appearance; make them part of your periodic assessments.

- *Practice handling breakdowns by using exercises and role-playing.*

  It's always best to develop your skills for handling emotional situations at times that are not emotionally charged. This can enable you to act from a place of power in the world rather than resignation.

Role-play can be a lighthearted and effective way to deal with emotions and develop skills with humor. Another very helpful approach would be to use the Responsibility Process program by Christopher Avery that I mentioned earlier. He emphasizes that total responsibility and powerful accountability are not personality traits or moral qualities but are instead states of mind and processes we can learn.

You can visit my website for a free tip sheet with additional, specific guidelines for handling breakdowns effectively. www.groupalchemy.net/account.

Create Structure for Routine Assessments

Committing to routine assessments can help everyone stay on track while eliminating the pressure to address every instance of success or failure at all times. Periodically taking a little time out of the usual day-to-day hustle of getting the job done to review how you're doing will help accelerate your results. Routinely assessing accountability to agreements about conduct gives members in the group important feedback during times that won't be charged with frustration over breakdowns.

Regular progress reports on performance give people a chance to share current performance status, celebrate success, and ask for help. Accountability for accomplishing goals and results is usually clear and straightforward when the goals are sufficiently specific and appropriate measures are put in place. Useful reporting mechanisms such as charts, dashboards (electronic data summaries for tracking progress on goals), and periodic reports help individuals and the group stay attuned to progress and make any needed course corrections. Varieties of these can be used daily, at weekly meetings, quarterly, and during annual reviews as appropriate. Visual metrics for group goals are great because they really help keep results in focus and can promote enthusiasm when progress is plain to see. We will discuss including an annual accountability assessment as a part of your renewal practice in chapter 5.

Accountability: Lessons Learned

Group success is impossible without accountability. Honest accounting is the bedrock of trust and confidence in relationships and is at the heart of what works in groups.

Sure, we can say, "We're grownups here. Everyone *should* act with integrity and be responsible." But we all know that's not what always happens, and it makes no sense to leave something so important to chance. Many of our organizations are set up in ways that don't model or support responsibility and accountability. How can we expect the highest moral capacity in the absence of an environment that nurtures it?

Powerful groups have conscious mechanisms for accountability—tied to their inspiration and agreements, clearly understood, and consistently applied. The do not allow a lack of accountability to corrode their inspiration and trust in one another.

The more consistently you practice accountability in low-stakes situations, such as what time your meetings start or agreements about sharing information, the more powerful your practices will be when you need them for more critical or stressful times. It is through routines and habits that you can maintain a culture that values integrity and builds trust.

This is group alchemy: a culture sparked by conscious inspiration and structured on agreements with total accountability. It is in this context that the specific habits that produce powerful accountability can be established.

Enhancing Accountability through Acknowledgment

Part of the promise of being accountable is that we will be recognized for successful outcomes and keeping our commitments. Instances where actions match commitments are great opportunities for *acknowledgment*—the recognition and reward that nourish further accountability. This is the subject of the next chapter and the next element in group alchemy.

Resources

The Oz Principle: Getting Results Through Individual and Organizational Accountability, Roger Connors, Tom Smith, Craig Hickman, Penguin Group, 2004.

"How, When, and Why Bad Apples Spoil the Barrel: Negative Group Members and Dysfunctional Groups," Will Felps, Terrence R. Mitchell and Eliza Byington, in *Research in Organizational Behavior*, Volume 27: 175–222, 2006.

Practical Wisdom: The Right Way to Do the Right Thing, Barry Schwartz and Kenneth Sharpe, Riverhead, 2010.

Responsibility Process, Christopher Avery, http://www.christopheravery.com/responsibility-process

The Speed of Trust, Stephen M. R. Covey, Free Press, 2006.

Winning With Accountability: The Secret Language of High-Performing Organizations, Henry J. Evans, Cornerstone Leadership Institute, 2008.

The 85% Solution: How Personal Accountaibility Guarantees Success, Linda Galindo, Jossey-Bass, 2009.

Element Four:

Acknowledgment

Reward excellence

Nourish confidence and optimism

Inspire the future

Encouragement sweetens labor.
—Jamaican proverb

As a result of your diligent work in the first three steps of the group alchemy formula, your foundation for success is now well established. What you stand for and the results you want to achieve are well defined in your inspiring stories. You now have agreements in place that structure how you will work together and what you can expect from each other. And you are engaging in routine practices to account for the group's activities, learn what works and what doesn't, and make any necessary corrections and adjustments.

Now it's time to turn your attention to how to reward the best of your efforts and achievements and keep your culture focused on what works.

In chapter 1 on inspiration you learned the importance of staying focused on the values and vision that underlie what you want to create. We all know how easy it is to dwell in the territory of tending to and preventing problems; they practically scream for our attention. But while problems need solutions, focusing primarily on weakness and insufficiency can only take us so far. It cannot sustain the creative initiative to improve, achieve, and excel.

Instead, powerful groups amplify their inspiration and support their agreements by emphasizing what's going well. They seize opportunities to recognize and express gratitude for each group member's special talents, qualities, and contributions. They reward and celebrate the fruit of their efforts. This is the role of acknowledgment.

The importance of acknowledgment, ironically, often goes unacknowledged! It's easily disregarded as "soft" or too "touchy-feely"—as though it has no bearing on performance and results—and is consequently undeveloped in the group's culture. This chapter remedies this misconception by revealing acknowledgment as a fundamental element of effectiveness. Following the principles and practices found here will ensure that you know how to give acknowledgment its rightful place in your culture.

The acknowledgment task of powerful groups is
to demonstrate appreciation for those contributions that support
the group's purpose, identity, and goals.

Recognizing Contribution and Affirming Value

Acknowledgment refers to all forms of appreciation, gratitude, and rewards for work well done. These include monetary compensation, promotions in status, verbal expressions of gratitude, and award ceremonies.

We all need encouragement. It helps us remain optimistic and motivated. Nothing inspires and encourages us more than knowing that our accomplishments are noticed and appreciated, whether we've landed a hundred-thousand-dollar contract or simply kept a discussion on track during a meeting. But what makes such good feelings an element of the alchemy of powerful groups?

It's helpful to distinguish acknowledgement from compliments. Complimenting someone—praising a new outfit or admiring a golf swing—is a nice thing to do and builds good feelings. It contributes to a positive experience, and can in turn contribute to good results.

But the role acknowledgment plays in a group's success is about much more than being nice and making people feel good. It's about recognizing and validating what serves the group's purpose *in terms the group has defined*. This means that acknowledgment is directly linked to the group's inspiration and agreements. While a personal compliment strengthens the bond between two people, acknowledgment that is tied to the group's mission and goals strengthens the identity and purpose within the group.

When you acknowledge specific ways people help the group keep its commitments, you affirm and amplify the group's values. And by doing that, you define and strengthen the culture through which people choose their future actions. This makes acknowledgment a corollary to accountability; both steer people in the direction of what works. For example, saying "Nice job" is helpful, but saying "The level of detail you included in that report made it easy to understand the implications for our budget" speaks to the value the "nice job" has brought to the group's objective of producing results. It makes explicit what really works, and that makes it easier to know how to repeat it.

Note that the underpinnings of acknowledgment are core values: the drivers of all that we do. Compliments, rewards, and appreciation are always about affirming values; there's nothing new there. What is available from the practice of *alchemical acknowledgment*—which explicitly expresses how actions have aligned with group values and commitments—is an increased level of performance and group cohesion.

At a workshop I gave recently, one executive put it this way: "If I say to an employee that I appreciate the quality of her report, I've made her feel good and increased the connection between her and me. If I say that the quality of the report enhances our ability to make the right decisions in our planning, I've strengthened her connection to the whole organization and its mission too."

The key is to *make sure that acknowledgment happens*—routinely, spontaneously, authentically, and generously. It can take verbal or written form, be monetary or not, but it has to be communicated. If we have appreciative thoughts but do not pass them along, we miss the opportunity to build the relationships that are essential to creating the future we want to see.

Acknowledgment Gets Results

David Yamada saw the benefits of acknowledgment when he directed the Public Interest Law Fund at New York University, whose purpose was to raise money for public-interest law projects and provide small grants to NYU students. He knew it could be challenging to keep a mix of students, faculty, professional lawyers, and nonprofit professionals in sync and that rifts could easily form along lines of institutional or social status. He was particularly aware of the potential for students to feel marginalized. Yet David knew that each person was invaluable to the group's cause, so he made acknowledgment a habit in their group.

The group had a good foundation because members shared a strong sense of purpose. David worked to help people connect to that through their unique talents so they could contribute in ways that suited them. Then he made a point of acknowledging those distinct talents and contributions in two ways: He made sure that everyone's views were heard in meetings. "We worked hard to listen to each other" he told me, even at times when there were strong disagreements. He also routinely took time in meetings to verbally express appreciation for everyone's presence and their particular contributions.

During his leadership, the organization was able to revive a lapsed fundraising program and give the largest grants in its history.

Two Domains

By the time we have arrived at this step in the group alchemy formula, it's clear that in each element sustained success comes from attention to results in both mission-specific tasks *and* group-building behaviors. It comes as no surprise, then, that acknowledgment is needed in both areas as well.

I think it's safe to say that recognizing people for their accomplishments in performing mission-related tasks is well established in our society. This variety of recognition includes monetary rewards such as salaries, bonuses, and fringe benefits. It can also be expressed through special awards, taking a moment to recognize important accomplishments during a group meeting, presenting a token such as a certificate of appreciation, or providing a prized parking space to the employee of the month.

Much less recognized or publicly praised are the ways in which people contribute to *how well the group works together*. And we have seen repeatedly that how people behave in the group and whether they support the group's agreements are as vital to overall results as the tasks they perform.

I know from my decades of doing this work that people *care* about this aspect of collaborating in a group—it is intrinsically important to them. Disregarding the quality of relationships and the collaboration itself for the sake of a mistaken, singular emphasis on performance of tasks ignores a crucial aspect of constructive results on the one hand, and the well-being and satisfaction everyone desires on the other. Without that feeling of well-being, what's the point of working in a group? This, unfortunately, is exactly what a lot of people ask themselves as they head into work.

The Cultural Link

Remember that people everywhere seek a sense of belonging and purpose. Acknowledgment is a critical link to both.

In anthropology we have learned from different societies around the world that people are motivated by much more than money or other material rewards. We refer to a "prestige economy" to describe what we see people everywhere pursue: recognition and prestige accorded by the people closest to them—their community. This is a direct reflection of what the group values and who it recognizes as successful in those terms. It so happens that in Western society money and accumulation are highly valued and thus linked to status and prestige. But this is not always the case. In many societies generosity is valued much more than accumulation of material wealth. The drive for status is such a powerful influence, in fact, that we find that the person with the highest status and prestige in those societies is the least materially wealthy; giving and sharing are so highly valued that he's given everything he owns away.

When we practice acknowledgment in the group alchemy way, by showing appreciation for actions that are tied to the group's collective inspiration and mutual agreements, we are creating a prestige economy, based on shared values and commitments, that is a powerful driver of behavior. We are working with the power of culture.

The Alchemy of Acknowledgment

Let's examine the ways acknowledgment is inherently culture building. You can think of acknowledgment as continually drawing attention to what success looks like. When a member of the group is being acknowledged, the words and ideas of inspiration stories come alive in shared experience and connect group members to their culture.

More specifically, acknowledgment serves group success in the following ways.

It Reinforces Inspiration

Practicing acknowledgment is one of the ways people stay in touch with their inspiration and keep from getting bogged down in problem solving. It is essentially another opportunity for creating a personal *experience* of shared inspiration—and we know from our discussion in chapter 1 that inspiration lives in experience. In this way acknowledgment reinforces the connection between individual motivations and the group goals forged in its inspiration practices.

It Strengthens Group Cohesiveness

When we express acknowledgment for the actions of another, we are acclaiming our mutual support for what we value. This is why both giving and receiving acknowledgment can feel so good. Acknowledgment is a way of connecting with others around what we care most about. It increases our sense of belonging. It's powerful between two people, and when it occurs in the group, it is even more potent.

Leadership Note

The current emphasis on leadership as a personal skill makes it easy for formal leaders to fall into the habit of using acknowledgment to build personal allegiance. But as the executive director I quoted earlier concerning the value of a good report realized, it's important for him to reinforce a sense of service to the group and organization, not to him as an individual. This can take diligence. We all have a desire to enhance our status in the eyes of others. Bestowing compliments is one way of doing that, so it's easy to be seduced into heightening the interpersonal relationship and losing sight of the bigger picture.

It Reinforces Agreements

When people acknowledge each other for the specific ways in which they support the group's process and for keeping agreements, they reinforce those agreements—and the positive behavior that supports them. This is part of the process of maintaining the cultural standards that reduce the likelihood of negative or inappropriate behavior.

It Inspires Future Excellence

Because acknowledgment references something that has already happened, we tend to think it's about the past. But when we show appreciation for what someone has done, we inspire them to do more of it. In this way the real value of acknowledgment is in inspiring the future. Think about the last time someone whose values you share acknowledged you for something you did well. Didn't it make you want to do more of it and repeat that experience?

As we have already established, the focus on what's working, not on what's wrong, is a stance that works. Inspiration dies in isolation but thrives in relationships. Response and recognition create an atmosphere of confidence and optimism—both inspiring qualities. This is a creative space.

Learning and Improvement Evolve Naturally

Acknowledgment is an important key to learning and performance. By providing positive feedback, we provide information about what works—instilling confidence and reinforcing that behavior. Such information can also inspire improvement. When we hear about what we did well, such as the attention we gave a client, it can help us see other instances where we have not lived up to that (overlooking a way we could have helped solve a problem for another client, perhaps) and make adjustments.

The information available through acknowledgment can also help people identify their strengths and the best places to apply them. People do their best work when they are expressing their personal strengths. Acknowledgment can encourage that fit.

You Get Better Results

Being acknowledged for your efforts improves your state of mind and contributes to feeling happy and fulfilled. There is no question that such feelings of well-being improve results. Consider the implications for your own work of this research cited by psychologist Christine Carter in her book *Raising Happiness:*

Doctors put in a positive mood before sitting down with a patient make accurate diagnoses 19 percent faster than those in a neutral state.

Managers who acknowledge their employees just one additional time each day can raise productivity 31 percent.

Students who are told something positive before taking tests do better on those tests.

Accountability Is Built In

Acknowledging someone's contribution is a form of accountability; when the assessment step of accountability is positive, the appropriate response is acknowledgement. If we know that accountability will lead to significant acknowledgment where appropriate, it can be easier to face accounting that leads to correction.

People Experience Satisfaction and Fulfillment

Acknowledgment communicates that individuals' contributions are significant. They feel noticed and valued. This supports a positive and creative environment for the individual and the whole group. The esteem, collegiality, good will, and sense of belonging in the group that acknowledgment provides generate much of the fulfillment people seek from their groups.

Health Improves

Research by the Institute of HeartMath shows that heartfelt emotions such as love, care, *appreciation*, and compassion create healthy heart rhythms and body chemistry. Both the giver and receiver of appreciation enjoy these benefits. In a cohesive group, I think it would be safe to say that everyone who witnesses the acknowledgment receives them too. The ultimate benefits of these improvements in body chemistry are enhanced learning, improved memory, and expanded creativity.

The Cost When Acknowledgment Is Weak

It is not difficult to imagine what lack of acknowledgment costs because most of us have experienced it at some time in our lives, some of us far too often. Think back to the last time you felt taken for granted or unappreciated. It can be demoralizing—painful even. In work groups, this emotional response leads to a serious loss in productivity that manifests in several ways.

People lose inspiration and imagination. Without the nourishment acknowledgment provides, creativity and initiative wane. Motivation languishes.

Recognition thrives in reciprocity; each act of acknowledgment inspires another. Generosity is the result. In a paucity of appreciation, people tend to hunker down to protect their own interests. Lack of recognition brings out insecurity and pettiness. *People become stingy and territorial.*

Certitude, a sense of accomplishment, and self-esteem develop when we get feedback about what works. Without it, we have to generate these states on our own and in a vacuum—if we can find the wherewithal to do so. More commonly, we withdraw for protection, and this leads to *a culture of mediocrity*. When we aren't acknowledged for our actions, we don't aspire to excellence and *results deteriorate*.

As is the case with weakness in every element of group alchemy, the ultimate impact is that *talented people leave*. They will go where they feel seen and appreciated. Study after study shows that feeling overlooked and unappreciated is one of the top reasons people leave their jobs, always ranking ahead of the amount of pay. The most talented people have the best alternative options, so this leaves your group with those who may have the least to offer your vision and goals or who are uninspired or unmotivated because they feel neglected.

Reflection Questions

1. How would you describe the health of acknowledgment practices in your group?

2. Do members of the group feel appreciated and recognized? Is this true across the organization or are there differences between different segments of the organization?

3. How have you prioritized acknowledgment in your group? In your leadership practice?

4. Describe how your group's formal structure for acknowledgment links to your values and agreements.

Principles of Acknowledgment Practice

We have already established that acknowledgment is an expression of core values, and that for it to be an element of group alchemy it needs to be more than a compliment by being linked to the group's mission. Powerful acknowledgment practice is further enhanced by incorporating the following principles.

Principle 1: Acknowledgment Is Specific

The more specific you can make your acknowledgments, the more powerful they will be. Generalities don't go very far in validating someone's efforts and they do not provide much information about what behaviors should be repeated.

Here is a good example from a client with a small medical practice who recently hired a new receptionist.

> **"Here's What I Value about Your Work"**
> At the end of his receptionist's probation period, the doctor I worked with took her to lunch to celebrate her transition to permanent status. He took the time to speak in detail, and used specific examples to acknowledge her efficiency in scheduling, her ability to anticipate and prevent problems, and her tact and courtesy with patients—all outstanding personal qualities that he values highly and wants to encourage in her and everyone in the office because they make a significant contribution to the success of the practice. This doctor's clarity about what he values translated beautifully into meaningful acknowledgment. The receptionist was grateful for the specific feedback and continues to be a stellar member of the team. And she expresses similar acknowledgment to her coworkers, further helping to develop the effectiveness of the whole group.

Principle 2: Acknowledgment Is Authentic

For acknowledgment to work powerfully, it has to be a genuine expression of appreciation. Gratitude is a positive emotion that builds relationships. It is identifiable by a sense of goodwill and satisfaction, even happiness. It is focused on the recipient, with no strings attached.

Note that acknowledgment is distinct from flattery, which is tied to a personal agenda, given in order to get something in return. It is ultimately about the speaker, not the receiver, and certainly not about a group's purpose or success. This amounts to the difference between a personal agenda and a commitment to the group. It's the difference between "I want you to do what I want" and "I want the group (us) to succeed."

You can't manipulate acknowledgment to get the results you want. People are very sensitive to insincerity and the impersonal masked as personal. In her book *All Work and No Say*, Jody Urquhart points out that "trite and generic compliments" often backfire and create distrust and cynicism. An example of this would be a general statement like "Thanks to everyone for working over the weekend to get this project done" without any expression of the particular quality of the work, its relationship to the overall goals the group has been focused on, or any recognition for what people gave up personally to be there over the weekend. It becomes especially trite if people feel passed over for raises or promotions, or simply never hear a personal acknowledgment from their boss.

A Common Stumbling Block: No Feelings Allowed

Most corporate culture is based on a premise that feelings get in the way of accomplishments, that they are unprofessional and must be minimized in the workplace. This is, of course, a fabrication built on denial; in reality, feelings are always present.

Because of this cultural propensity to minimize feelings, many professional men and women lack practice in acknowledgment and feel uncomfortable with it. They fear they will appear soft, not powerful.

I hope this discussion helps counteract such ideas. Acknowledgment based on genuine feelings of appreciation is a powerful engine of success and the mark of great leaders.

Principle 3: Acknowledgment Is a Tribute

Constructive acknowledgment expresses respect and gratitude for what another has done in support of our shared values. It arises from our shared identity. It is not fundamentally about judgment: "I judge you to have done well." If you have ever felt patronized when being complimented, you understand the distinction. If I compliment you from a mindset of being right, my compliment can feel condescending. When I express my appreciation for the way in which you affirm what we hold in common and what we stand for, then I pay tribute to you.

Principle 4: Acknowledgment Is Customary— and It's Spontaneous

By customary I refer to routine mechanisms for acknowledgment that have become the custom in the organization or group. This includes formal reward systems—every paycheck expresses acknowledgment—as well as awards given at certain times or for particular levels of service. Annual sales meetings that reward performance and anniversary parties are examples.

Routine acknowledgment could also be the habit of taking the first ten minutes of a staff meeting for people to share "goods and news" so that everyone has a chance to recognize significant accomplishments in the previous period. One of my clients hands out a special certificate at weekly staff meetings that says congratulations and then tells everyone what the recipient did and explains the significance to the entire group of the individual's accomplishment. Having customs such as these helps make sure that acknowledgment happens regularly and in a timely way. It encourages people to make note of and remember recognition-worthy moments.

Acknowledgment also needs to occur spontaneously—as the spirit moves you. When something great happens, talk about it then. If someone makes a helpful contribution during a meeting, acknowledge it on the spot. When you get an email or a report from a colleague that really helps you out, go ahead and call, text, email, or cross the office to tell them you appreciate it. Celebrate the good. Capture that enthusiasm.

Principle 5: Acknowledgment Is Shared

"The more the merrier" holds true when it comes to acknowledgment. Recognizing someone's efforts one-to-one is good, but it's even better when shared in the group. There is something in it for everyone: the speaker, the receiver, and the group. Giving, receiving, and witnessing acknowledgment all create powerful experiences of shared purpose and meaning.

Principle 6: Acknowledgment Is Personal

People vary in what inspires them and makes them feel well recognized, so the particular form acknowledgment takes might need to be customized according to the recipient. One person might appreciate a cash bonus while another might prefer a few extra days off from work to be with their family. It might mean a lot for one person to be recognized in the organization's newsletter while another might feel more valued by a personal moment of recognition from the boss. It's important to take the time to learn what is meaningful to members of your group.

Research indicates that there are cultural and gender differences in the practice and comfort zone of acknowledgment. This fact, as is the case with all of the elements of group alchemy, means that it is necessary to discuss acknowledgement: what it means to each member of your group and how *your* group will create its own meaningful acknowledgement practices.

> **Informal Leadership**
> As a member of any group, you can easily begin to inspire it by using acknowledgement. Wherever the group's inspiration is clear and you see people fulfilling it, you can openly acknowledge it. This will create a positive climate—and you might be surprised by how contagious it is.

Principle 7: Acknowledgment Is Story

Acknowledgment is simply an expression of how we see things. It doesn't have to be objectively proven with scientific evidence. Can you prove the value to your mission of someone's sense of humor? No. Yet you can feel quite confident that it is invaluable to your team's success.

Don't get hung up on "getting it right": *What if I missed something? Maybe what this person did isn't as good as I think it is or as it could be. It's better not say anything until I'm sure that everyone agrees.* Some people have told me that this is what makes them hesitant to acknowledge. This is a trap. Here's a story a colleague shared with me.

"I can't think of anything..."

As the clinical director for a major university medical program, Roland was facilitating an all-faculty planning meeting. He began the meeting by saying, "Let's review how we did over the past year. What are our triumphs and successes?"

He was met with a "resounding silence." Surprised by this, he spent fifteen minutes struggling to get the group to acknowledge its accomplishments. The twenty-four group members finally created a list of three things. He saw this struggle as a consequence of being so focused on critique and analysis that they were uncomfortable acknowledging things as going well. They are not a very cohesive team.

Acknowledgment is not an assessment against an absolute standard of good or bad. My assessment of the value of someone's contribution might be different from yours. If I take ownership for how I see that contribution and what I value about it, I don't have to be worried about "getting it right." I can express my appreciation for whatever contribution I see.

Practices for Powerful Acknowledgment

As with each of the elements of group alchemy, time spent developing your practices in acknowledgment will be returned to you many times over in the forms of improved results and greater well-being. Good habits need support and structure to develop. This can be especially important with acknowledgment to ensure that it doesn't get forgotten in the rush, or become rote and meaningless.

Conduct an Acknowledgment Assessment

Assess the status of acknowledgment in your group by answering these questions.

- When and where do you find acknowledgment happening in your group?
- What kind of acknowledgment do you observe happening spontaneously? What are your routine acknowledgment practices?
- How are you acknowledging the contributions people make to your most important commitments? Your goals? Your agreements?
- Does your reward structure support your values and commitments?
- Do your members feel appreciated? Does this vary across departments or segments of your organization?

Practice Giving Acknowledgment

As I mentioned earlier in the chapter, acknowledgment doesn't come naturally to everyone. It can be downright challenging for some people because as a society we don't have enough experience doing it. You can develop this skill through practice, however. Before you know it your group will have built strong "acknowledgment muscles." A few examples follow.

Cultivate appreciation in your personal style. If acknowledgment is not your personal habit, it can help if you start with people you are most comfortable with and then extend outward from there. Judith Umlas gives some suggestions for ways to develop your own habits in her book *The Power of Acknowledgment*.

Conduct group exercises to help everyone practice. Be playful. I have seen people who were initially uncomfortable with this respond powerfully to these exercises and create a palpable shift in their group. Go to www.groupalchemy.net/acknowledge for an exercise to get you started.

Give Acknowledgment Powerfully

Use these guidelines for giving acknowledgment.

- Take responsibility for your perception of what the person has done that you think is of value: say "I."

- Make it personal: say "you" or the person's name.

- Be explicit about how the action/behavior served the group's *goals and mission*.

- Focus on specific, concrete, observable behaviors, as opposed to general, abstract personality qualities that are inferred from behavior.

In practice, these guidelines result in statements such as the following:

- "I appreciate the clear and concise feedback you gave me on the staffing report. It helped me to link our staffing plans with our goals more clearly."

- "I would like to acknowledge Terry for responding so quickly to my request for information for the project proposal. It really helped me complete it on time."

- "Javier, when you stopped us to raise questions about whether we were on task I was surprised at first. Now I realize that you saved us a lot of time by keeping us from getting distracted."

- "Sonia, your sense of humor keeps us going, even in these difficult times of budget cuts."

Practice Receiving Acknowledgment Powerfully

Practice receiving acknowledgment by saying "Thank you." Full stop. Receive it. Let it sink in.

Many of us have a hard time receiving acknowledgment. This might be because we haven't understood how important the act of acknowledgment is for all involved, or we think it's polite to demur, or we suffer from an underlying belief that we are not worthy. So we respond by saying, "Oh, it was nothing, really" or "I didn't really do it—it was Sam who made it work."

When you're tempted to do this, here's something important to keep in mind: when we shy away from or rebuff compliments, we essentially refuse a gift and dismiss the connection being offered. We miss the chance to share an experience of our values. We are in effect, saying, "Oh no, you're wrong" and risk *diminishing the person offering the gift*.

Remember: receiving acknowledgment is validating for the giver as well as the receiver. When you view it in this light you can see that this minimizing response serves to dampen the habit of appreciation and the generative power it has. We have already established that acknowledgment is not about precise analysis, but is instead a story about how we perceive and interpret what others have done. You can accept it as such and enjoy it.

Create a Structure for Acknowledgment

Acknowledgment should be spontaneous and frequent—and like all good habits, acknowledgment needs a structure to support it. Having structure for special acknowledgment times will help you build your skills in spontaneously responding to recognition-worthy moments. Here are some things to try:

- Look at your inspiration statements—your core values, vision, mission, goals—and your group agreements for ideas about specific actions and behavior that you will want to acknowledge. For instance, if your values statements place an emphasis on customer care, you'll want to stay alert for specific things people do that expresses that value. If your agreements include a commitment to mutual assistance and cooperation, you will want to develop acknowledgment of those behaviors.

- Commit to routine situations for acknowledgment events. These might include staff meetings, board meetings, periodic reviews, special events, wrap-up of special projects, and group transitions (seasonal, workflow, personnel, etc.). Put it on your agenda! That's a simple and sure-fire way to ensure that it happens. Then you can let people respond spontaneously.

- Try some playful approaches if that fits your personality or the group culture. Perhaps a mock Academy Awards ceremony, skits, role-playing, poems, or songs.

Thinking Globally, Acknowledging Locally

The university had a declared commitment to the highest quality in instruction. But it was clear that the formal reward structures of tenure and promotions that were in place for faculty focused almost exclusively on research and publishing, with scant attention to teaching. The quality of teaching was largely left up to the personal commitments and interest of individual faculty members.

There was widespread agreement that making substantial improvements in the quality of the educational experience for undergraduates would depend upon changes in the reward structure. This is difficult to do in a large, complex system that is tied to an international reward structure across academic professions. Linking salaries and promotions to teaching was not likely to occur in a substantial way. My research on that project showed that exciting improvements in teaching resulted from innovative approaches for rewarding such efforts at the local (departmental) level. Faculties were able to provide meaningful recognition, such as teaching awards, that operated at the level of the prestige economy we discussed earlier, as well as easing departmental workloads.

- You might create an acknowledgment committee. It can be charged with identifying personally meaningful ways people like to be acknowledged and doing periodic assessments about whether people feel acknowledged and whether your acknowledgment is tied to your inspiration.

- Pay particular attention to ways to acknowledge group members for their positive effect on the group—what I call "group building behaviors." Recall that there is chronic lack of attention to individual contributions to the *group performance*, so this is a practice that needs extra effort.

Be sure to keep it meaningful. Even while you create structure to keep acknowledgment on your agenda, don't allow it to become rote. The power is in staying responsive to the moment.

Create Effective and Appropriate Reward Structures

Formal rewards such as salaries, bonuses, and promotions are potent forms of acknowledgment. Given the significance of acknowledgment in general and the particular influence of these particular mechanisms on motivation, it is wise to give careful attention to the structure of these rewards so you can ensure that they support the results you seek. They must be consistent with the group's inspiration, support your agreements and accountability, and encourage learning and mastery (element six in the group alchemy system).

Be careful what you reward because you will surely get more of it. For instance, it's common to reward individual performance that encourages an individualistic outlook even while espousing a commitment to cooperation and teamwork. This is how those segregated islands (silos) develop in larger organizations. Such a lack of consistency can lead to various disconnects between results and mission. One lesson in this came to me while I was involved in a project for improving undergraduate education in the University of California system (see sidebar, next page).

I encourage you to explore some of the research and practices on how to create reward systems that foster collaboration and reward mutual learning. There has been much investigation into these questions with various approaches being tried to suit local situations.

For instance, consider salaries or bonuses that are tied to overall group (or organization-wide) results. Do people get rewarded for the group or organizational results, or just for their personal performance? Look at your promotion practices. Are you promoting people with little awareness of their impact on others and how they can contribute to the group's overall effectiveness? If you are promoting people for their technical skills but ignoring how they impact the quality of the group and its collaboration, you are in effect building a culture that detracts from your effectiveness. Or do you reward your members for taking responsibility to become facilitative leaders and foster the group's capacity? Do you include rewards for the specific ways people contribute to the efficiency of the group process?

A valuable resource on the subject of rewards and motivation is the book *Drive* by Daniel Pink. He synthesizes many decades of research about motivation that correlates with much of what we are practicing in group alchemy. A sense of purpose, self-completion, and enjoyment are more motivating and lead to great creativity than pure financial rewards.

Award Programs

Formal award programs are commonly used to acknowledge quality of performance beyond the standard reward/salary structure. Such a program can be a useful tool in an acknowledgment repertoire. Just be sure to develop it in ways that support genuine recognition and avoid the common pitfall of standardized, routine programs that become trivial. As Jody Urquhart points out, they can actually create resentment if the same top performers are recognized all the time, or if the reward is small in proportion to the accomplishment. In that case, genuine verbal recognition is more meaningful than a trivial financial award.

Acknowledgment: Lessons Learned

Acknowledgment is a creative act that can give an organization the extra horsepower it needs to achieve extraordinary results. Unfortunately, it's underappreciated and underdeveloped in most groups. If this is the case with your group, it is actually good news; you have vast untapped potential. Acknowledgment isn't hard and doesn't have to be expensive. You need only make it part of your group alchemy.

Recall that one of our greatest motivators is the esteem that others hold for us. You can build a prestige economy in your group that reinforces your values and commitments and capitalize on the power of culture. Of course I am not suggesting that you can do this in place of meaningful monetary compensation. It is not a matter of either one or the other. Doing both well is where you will gain value.

If you learn the principles of powerful acknowledgment and implement some of the practices you have just been introduced to, you can quickly and dramatically improve the atmosphere and culture of your group and the experience of everyone who participates in it. That will lead to much greater success.

Acknowledgment Energizes Renewal

The reinforcement and recognition that occur in acknowledgment are part of the process of renewing the group. Next we turn our attention to the fifth group alchemy practice, the practice of renewal.

Resources

All Work and No Say: How to Captivate Your Workforce, Boost Morale and Improve Productivity, Jody Urqhart, Iconoclast Publishing, 2004.

Drive: The Surprising Truth About What Motivates Us, Daniel H. Pink, Riverhead Books, 2009.

Encouraging the Heart: A Leader's Guide to Rewarding and Recognizing Others, James M. Kouzes and Barry Z. Posner, Josey-Bass, 2003.

Institute of HeartMath, www.heartmath.org.

The Power of Acknowledgment, Judith Umlas, International Institute for Learning, 2007.

Raising Happiness, Christine Carter, Ballantine Books, 2010.

Recognition, Gratitude, and Celebration, Patrick L. Townsend and Joan E. Gebhardt, American Society for Quality, 2007.

Element Five:

Renewal

Foster innovation

Sustain the group's energy

Navigate change with confidence

It's not the strongest of the species that survives, nor the most intelligent,
but the one most responsive to change.
—Charles Darwin

A s you have progressed through this book I have encouraged you to create good habits in each of the first four elements of group alchemy. In doing so I've drawn upon the natural tendency of humans and groups to form habits. This tendency can be a good thing because once we figure out which actions work for us, it's efficient to repeat them. Such routines help us get to work on time, keep the bills paid, and file the month-end reports accurately.

And, like every good thing, they have a downside. If we don't break out of patterns from time to time to evaluate them, they can become hindrances. This is because life entails change, and we must be ready to respond to it; the habits we develop to fit one set of circumstances may prove useless in other. Have you ever changed jobs and then suddenly found yourself automatically driving to your old workplace one morning?

In terms of groups, this downside is illustrated by the fact that habits that are effective in a young organization might be less so as it matures: entrepreneurial organizations often possess a distinct cultural environment that no longer serves when the group becomes an established industry leader. Changes in the size and scale of the group also influence which practices it needs to adopt; more formal structures and procedures, for example, often follow increases in size. Changes in the external environment can also induce dramatic changes inside a group, forcing it to adapt or risk becoming irrelevant.

Groups, like individuals, have varying capacities for anticipating and responding to change. Powerful groups embrace it and deliberately create the conditions that will facilitate changing their habits when needed. In this way they build flexibility into their culture so they can readily adapt and stay inspired. This is the promise of renewal.

This chapter explains the nature of renewal in groups and how to create positive practices that will keep your group responsive to change *and* focused on your core values and goals.

The renewal task of powerful groups is to routinely evaluate and develop practices and rituals that refresh the group's commitments, foster improvements, and respond to change.

Harness the Power of Conscious Renewal

Brilliance is so rare because it is always obstructed,
often by the very stuff that keeps us so busy.
—Scott Belsky

Renewal refers to the fundamental life cycle of completion and new beginning. This cycle happens continually in the natural world—and in social groups. In groups, the cycle of renewal occurs through the actions and interactions of their members. You are renewing your group culture all the time through what you do and say. This is a familiar theme by now as we have explored how your actions in each element form your culture.

And this gives renewal its dual nature: it happens automatically through your actions and interactions *and* you have the opportunity to consciously engage this cultural dynamic and renew your culture in positive ways that enhance the conditions for your success.

Remember the discrepancy between ideal culture and real culture. Given that we are creating and reproducing our culture all the time, it behooves us to become alert to exactly what we are creating. For instance, if your group says that it values new ideas but every time someone brings one forward it gets shot down as unrealistic, then your real culture is one of little openness to new ideas. Furthermore, the fact that you say one thing yet do another is now also part of your culture. This kind of situation directly influences how people understand the group and how they choose their behavior, and that means you might be routinely recreating what you don't want.

The renewal practices described here will help you to stay ahead of this problem. If you don't like the results you're getting, trace back to find what you're doing that creates those results. Then you can adjust your practices accordingly, renew your inspiration and commitments, and support your group's development. This is the conscious practice of renewal.

As an element of group alchemy *renewal* refers to the set of practices that enable you to continually re-create your group to stay aligned with your values and goals. These practices include reviewing and assessing your actions and your outcomes, affirming or revising as appropriate, celebrating your successes, and planning for your future. Here you reconnect to your purpose, goals, and agreements and refresh your best practices. You change what doesn't work and adjust to new conditions. Renewal also involves reconstituting the group in response to transitions and changes as well as orienting and enculturating new members.

Change is constant and inevitable—planned and unplanned and both internal and external. It requires continuous adjustment of the system to ensure survival. Successful

Cycle of Renewal

Take Stock

Acknowledge
Transitions
and Passages

Affirm
What Works

Plan

Revise

Celebrate Success
and Pay Tribute

Prune or
Eliminate

organizations are adaptive systems, constantly taking in new information, assessing the system's ability to respond, and making adjustments as needed.

A systematic renewal process—with special opportunities to pause and assess how you're doing in terms of your values, vision, goals, and agreements—benefits every group. This is important because the focus necessary for accomplishing day-to-day business can cause you to lose the "peripheral vision" that enables you to see the wider world as it changes and to recognize the forces that are likely to shape the future. It's not easy to break from the routine of getting things done in order to observe what's working or not working, nor is it easy to look up from the path you're on and rigorously question your assumptions and habits in order to test their effectiveness. I've had many clients who felt they could not afford the luxury of taking time to do a review-and-assessment process, yet it was precisely this that would help them break the logjam they were in and move to greater levels of efficiency.

This element, like the others, will likely call you to create some new practices. At the same time, conscious renewal includes a lot of things you probably already do. You are *positively* renewing your group any time you engage in a process to identify and claim what worked and what didn't, make needed adjustments, and affirm your successes. Let's look at a few of the ways this occurs.

Practices that routinely create opportunities to broaden your perspective will help keep you from getting stuck in unproductive habits. The more established and inviolable your renewal practices, the less likely your group will be to get swept along in the pressures of daily demands and miss its greatest opportunity for improvement. Your group can be proactive instead of merely responding to events and changing conditions. New insights find room to emerge, and you create new possibilities.

The following story of Brighton House provides a good example.

Reconnecting with Mission

Brighton House asked me to help them with their strategic planning process.
At our first meeting the board was concerned about the fact that their program activity had drifted away from their original mission. Brighton House was created to provide residential recovery assistance to people in the local community with substance addictions. Over the previous several years, they had developed a large program for parolees from the state prison a hundred miles away who had been discharged into a mandatory drug rehabilitation program. These clients were not originally from the local area but they came with state funding for the program. The parolee program made sense at first; that money helped Brighton House meet overhead expenses in ways that supported their underfunded programs for local residents. But over time the scope of the parolee programs had begun to overtake services for local residents. The attraction of the funding had lured them away from their core mission.

They had become torn between the need for money to stay afloat and their core values of providing for the needs of their local community. The parolees' needs for help with addiction recovery was connected to that part of Brighton House's core mission, so they felt a lot of satisfaction from the good work they were able to do in that regard. It took some time to review all the angles and resolve differing points of view in the group. Gradually it became clear that they were off their mission and that their first commitment was to the local community.

The time they spent in planning meetings reconnecting with their core values helped them renew their commitment to their mission. They didn't want to change who they were; they wanted to change what they were doing so it once again reflected their focus on the local community. They gradually reorganized their programs, partnered with other local organizations to combine efforts, developed new strategies for raising funds to support the programs for local residents, and reduced the size of and their dependence on the state parolee program.

Renewal in Everyday Moments

Renewal occurs in everyday moments, such as during regular staff meetings when you pause to assess or celebrate how you're doing. This might be as simple as asking, "How is our new product launch going?" or "How do you think our fundraiser went?"

Setting aside some time in regular meetings for such open reflection and evaluation is a renewing practice. You can do this routinely. It can also be especially valuable after important events. The group gets time to join in interpreting their significance.

The higher you go on the organizational ladder, the harder this can be because there are such powerful, immediate demands on executive time. Yet this makes it all the more important because it is from this kind of socializing that people establish the shared understanding, trust, and coherence that support real collaboration. And that's exactly what you need when facing the kinds of big, difficult challenges that confront executive groups.

Resolution Renews

One of the most damaging things groups do is avoid dealing with sensitive issues. In doing so, they essentially create their group as dishonest, fearful, or uncommitted. Resolving difficult issues in the group provides powerful renewal because these elephants in the room distract you from achieving your potential; secrets, avoidance, and discomfort pull people away from inspiration. Agreements are threatened. But as soon as you acknowledge the elephant, talk about it, and resolve it, you reestablish coherence and positively renew your group.

Renewing the Agenda

One executive group I worked with frequently began its weekly meetings with lots of discussion about recent events, even though doing so was not on the agenda. They regularly spent twenty minutes or more talking about such things as what happened during the board meeting the night before or sharing stories about a special visitor who toured their operation the previous week.

This was the one time during the week when this entire group sat down together. They clearly hungered for the chance to share information informally, to socialize and celebrate together. But because they had not budgeted time for this in their meetings, the already packed agendas started late and they had less time to get their work done. Their meetings inevitably ended in a stressful scramble, often with someone's important agenda item getting put off until the following week.

As we worked in the renewal element and reviewed the effectiveness of their meetings, they decided to include time on their agendas for these discussions. Allotting time for this improved the quality of their meetings by honoring what was an important part of their group culture. They became more realistic about their agendas, which also meant they got better at keeping their agreements.

You've already developed some of these kinds of positive renewal practices as you've worked through the group alchemy formula thus far. For instance, by bringing values, vision, and mission into play when you're confronting problems and making decisions, you reinforce your group's purpose and collective resolve. When you practice acknowledgment, you're refreshing your inspiration and reaffirming your agreements. Every time you hold yourself accountable for doing what you said you would do, you renew your commitments. Similarly, when you resolve a breakdown in agreements or communication, you renew the power of your group.

Renewal in Special Events

In addition to everyday practices, periodic and special events can be renewing. These include practical goal-oriented activities such as strategic planning, program evaluation, and year-end reviews. Equally important are more social and symbolic activities such as organization-wide meetings, annual conferences, award ceremonies, and parties. New-member orientations and exit interviews for people leaving the organization also provide for renewal.

Special events are especially potent forms of renewal by virtue of the fact that they do not happen routinely; they are extraordinary. They also have special significance when they involve all or most members of the group because they reinforce the experience of the whole. Such collective activities as formal gatherings, ceremonies, and even weekly staff meetings function as *rituals* in the group.

Ritual doesn't always involve elaborate pageantry or religious rites; ritual is taking place—whether consciously or not—whenever you meet together. You are enacting your values and beliefs and reinforcing group identity as well as the individual roles of its members. You are reproducing and renewing your culture.

This can work for or against your stated aspirations for your work together; it depends on how you conduct your rituals. Lack of awareness and intention concerning what's happening in these "ceremonies" (meetings) can mean that you're reproducing a dysfunctional culture: one of inefficiencies and competition, or not doing what you say, or manipulation and petty arguments. You are ritually reproducing the *real* culture in your group, not necessarily your stated ideals.

This is why I consider the quality of meetings extremely important and why we should never settle for frustrating or ineffective meetings. Meetings deserve our utmost care and attention because they are *some of the most valuable opportunities* that exist to create your power as a group. Their impact reaches far beyond what you actually accomplish in any meeting.

To summarize the role of renewal, when you conduct your routine and special events so that you reconnect to your mission, goals, and agreements, you draw on the power

> ### Ritual Matters
>
> Just as all societies have had myths to explain their origins and how they should live, so all societies practice rituals to reconnect with their origins and experience their collective identity. Rituals are as central as myths to what it is to be human because they are ways groups reproduce themselves. They are symbolic enactments of the group's fundamental values and beliefs. As a central element of culture, ritual is already in play in your group, helping determine your outcomes. And it's an aspect of culture that you can develop further to support your success.
>
> Rituals are formalized activities regularly followed by a person or group. Their character is to be stereotyped, predictable, structured events or ceremonies that are repeated at regular times and places. Traditionally these were sacred ceremonies intended to reinforce the connection between the spiritual and worldly realms. Because they involve everyone (or nearly so), they serve to organize and integrate the society and produce a sense of solidarity as well as personal identity as a member of the group.
>
> While the early meaning of the world *ritual* was religious, it's used in a secular sense today, even as a synonym for *routine*. When the term is used in this way, the stereotyped and predictable aspects of ritual are emphasized. This is the aspect Jim Loehr and Tony Schwartz emphasize in their book, *The Power of Full Engagement*. They refer to the benefits of "positive energy rituals" (such as practice, fitness, diet, relaxation) for maintaining optimum performance at work, similar to what top athletes do. Their ideas draw on part of the traditional power of ritual.
>
> For our purposes here, it's helpful to also emphasize the *collective* dimension of participating in rituals. Even without sacred roots, the social functions of ritual—promoting solidarity and cohesion and reproducing core values and beliefs—remain.

of ritual to refresh your inspiration. You recreate your group culture in terms that truly match your purpose and achieve your goals. Then when you take the time to correct your course and revise or eliminate anything that doesn't serve your ideals, you ensure your effectiveness and make it sustainable. In that case, you can be confident you're doing all you can to create and maintain a group that serves your highest intentions.

We will look at renewal principles and practices in more depth later, but first let's consider the specific benefits that renewal offers groups.

The Alchemy of Renewal

> *We must always change, renew, rejuvenate ourselves; otherwise we harden.*
> —Johann von Goethe

Groups that are aware of the need for conscious renewal, know how it works, and create routine practices for it have a good chance of sustaining the energy, enthusiasm, and creativity they need to succeed over the long haul. Following are the results you will enjoy when you attend to this element of group alchemy with care.

People Act with Confidence and Clarity

The learning that comes from review and assessment allows for development and growth that instill confidence and enthusiasm. Having confidence that you know what's working and what isn't means you can make sure you have a mechanism to stay on course.

The Group Innovates

Research shows that creativity and learning need opportunity and time to emerge. The fresh ideas and consolidation of experience necessary for all group success depends on conscious encouragement. Renewal practices ensure an environment of expansiveness in which new ideas can blossom.

The Group Maintains Solidarity

Renewal practices that engage everyone and recall the group's inspiration foster solidarity by increasing connections among members. Reaffirming "who we are and what we are up to here" works to keep that inspiration vibrant and manifested in action. This is especially valuable where there are differences in points of view about the direction the group should take or where someone has an objection to how things are being done. Taking time to discuss and resolve these disagreements allows the members to affirm what they hold in common and come to agreements that support the collective purpose.

Enthusiasm Abounds

When people have opportunities to celebrate their success—in terms of both results and their effectiveness as a group—they reconnect with purpose and possibility. Periodically checking in and affirming what everyone is committed to reignites people's motivating spark to work hard for what they care about. This, along with celebrating success together, is crucial for keeping the group connected and inspired.

The Group Is Flexible and Adaptable

The learning that occurs as a result of the honest-assessment step of renewal strengthens the group's ability to revise its actions—or even change course when needed. Because this practice fosters listening closely to the environment and each other, it builds the group's capacity to adapt. This helps maintain a culture that defines mistakes and failures as opportunities for learning and improvement: a prerequisite for a climate that encourages change.

Success Is Sustainable

The evaluation and adaptation inherent in renewal mean you can recreate success no matter what changes occur in the environment. The consistent and systematic reconnection to purpose and inspiration keeps the group on track and nimble enough to adjust to changing reality.

The Cost When Renewal Is Weak

Failure to periodically take stock, reaffirm vision and purpose, integrate new members, renew commitments, and adjust plans will allow the group to grow stale and results to decline. Following are some of the pitfalls that active renewal practices can prevent.

If the group is a closed system, lacking opportunities to revitalize itself, many learning opportunities are lost, and the result is *stagnation*. The group hits a performance plateau and can't rise further, either in terms of results or group effectiveness.

A stagnant organization no longer speaks to the needs of the community or the marketplace and *the group loses relevance*.

Inspiration flags. People lose clarity about the group's goals. Mission drifts. Enthusiasm and the sense of connection fade and without them, people experience burnout. Without refreshment, revision, and rejuvenation, people become disillusioned and uninspired.

You may not be surprised to see *multi-headed beast syndrome* make a return. After all, if groups are not functioning well together—which happens when any element of group alchemy is weak—members have no choice but to go their own way. If there is no process to reach agreement about how to handle new opportunities or challenges presented by changes in the environment, members will pull in their own directions. Without the renewal practice of planning for the future, anxiety builds about what's going to happen next and individuals try to resolve their uncertainty by taking charge unilaterally.

As integrity concerning commitments breaks down and people give up, group members cease to believe in the group's possibilities; *cynicism prevails*.

Clear Mind, Strong Resolve

I worked with the founding codirectors of Community Resources for Science to develop their first strategic plan. They embraced the process fully and engaged an extensive planning process. Afterward they each described tremendous value from it. They appreciated knowing what their priorities were and knowing how their immediate activities led to the longer-term results they had committed to. They described how the clarity they got from having a detailed, well-thought out plan freed them from worry and "mental clutter." They could stay focused on daily priorities because they didn't always have to try to balance short- and long-term priorities. They had already done that in their planning process so they knew they were working in concert.

Without the renewal practice of airing unresolved differences, resentments simmer and people withdraw from one another. A *toxic environment* results. When new members enter this environment without committing to the group's inspiration and agreements, the *group culture degrades*.

The ultimate result of weakness in the renewal element is the same as weakness in each of the elements we have discussed before. *The group loses good people*, especially the most talented ones with the potential to make the strongest impact. And once that happens, it's nearly impossible to resurrect a high-functioning organization.

You can take advantage of all the benefits of a good renewal practice and avoid the serious drawbacks that crop up when it is weak or missing by consciously revitalizing your group.

Reflection Questions

1. Does your group routinely revisit your commitments in *inspiration* and *agreements* in order to reaffirm or revise them where needed? Do you use them as the basis for your evaluations and assessments of your progress?

2. Does your group routinely review your results and your process to assess the effectiveness of how you work together as a group? Do you make adjustments in your group process as a result of that review?

3. Do your meetings energize and unite everyone? Do they reflect your highest ideals? Do you have special events that serve to reinforce who you are and what you are up to?

Principles of Renewal Practice

Keeping the following principles in mind will help you to make the most of the activities during which group renewal already takes place and identify where you will benefit from adding activities.

As you do these things, you're creating traditions that can transmit your culture, purpose, and identity across the "generations" of your group. Not unlike homecoming games and alumni events in schools, your special practices that reconnect people to the group's purpose and history will reinforce its foundation and help new members join and build on its culture.

Principle 1: Renewal Means Reviewing and Assessing the Results Your Group Achieves and the Group's Effectiveness in Working Together

To build renewal into the fabric of your group, assess all aspects of the group's work together—on a predictable and routine basis, and as often as needed in between. Most organizations are accustomed to making assessments in terms of results. Including your inspiration and agreements in your assessments as well means that renewal will also reach into *how your group works together* to achieve those results. Let's look at each in turn.

Results

Rigorous, honest assessment is necessary to secure commitment and attract important resources. You need to use all available tools to get information about how you're doing. This evaluation can be part of strategic planning, market research, rebranding, or new-venture development. Annual reviews, program reviews, performance reviews, audits, climate assessments, and stakeholder focus groups are all possibilities. You can employ various diagnostic methods such as surveys, questionnaires, interviews, and focus groups, as appropriate.

Group Effectiveness

Assessing the group and its functioning also requires commitment and rigor. This practice is significantly underdeveloped in most groups for a very simple reason; no one has learned how to do it. Here, you are at a definite advantage. The first four elements of the group alchemy formula offer a comprehensive framework to help you evaluate how the group is working together in each one. Further ideas and tools for assessment are discussed in the practice section of this chapter.

Principle 2: Renewal Begins with Reaffirming Commitments

Periodically refreshing your commitment to your values, vision, mission, and goals is empowering for the group. Frequent opportunities to reconnect to your inspiration will keep the group energized and on track. The same is true for your group agreements. It's easy to lose sight of these in the hustle and bustle of daily activity. Positive declarations that affirm your ongoing commitments keep them alive.

Principle 3: Renewal Relies on Affirming What Works

When your assessment reveals strategies, practices, and habits that work to keep your group successful, it's valuable to affirm those by calling them out and acknowledging their role in your success. This reinforces them and makes them appealing.

Principle 4: Renewal Includes Celebrating Success

When the assessment phase of renewal indicates that things are working, celebrate! Don't take success for granted; articulate out loud what you did to create it. Remember a lesson from acknowledgment: this is about more than feeling good; it's also about organizational learning.

Principle 5: Renewal Requires Revising What Doesn't Work

> *The first draft reveals the art, revision reveals the artist.*
> —Michael Lee

When you identify weaknesses and actions that did not lead to success, you can change them. Eliminate things that flat-out need to go and make adjustments in those that could be improved.

Results

Let's look at this principle concerning results first. Do you have products that aren't profitable or programs that aren't effective? Get rid of what isn't working to free up time and energy for more fruitful action. Are you making money doing something that doesn't serve your mission? Then either change your mission or redirect your activities to align with it. Pruning and weeding are important habits in any endeavor.

Group Effectiveness

Renewal practice is partly housekeeping. In the context of how a group functions, housekeeping is about communication. It's very easy for garbage—misunderstandings, resentment, and distrust—to build up in any relationship between two people. Groups, with their multiple relationships and challenging tasks and responsibilities, are even more vulnerable to this. This means taking time to make sure that disagreements have been resolved and that there is no lingering residue of hurts or affronts. Inquire whether there is anything that has not been dealt with that needs resolution. By making sure there is no residual garbage lurking, you clear the way for creativity.

Don't assume that communication is clean even if no one is openly complaining. Every member of the group needs safe opportunities to reflect and resolve—to speak and be heard. This is a critical place where routines and systematic procedures are vital. Having an agreement about how to raise difficult issues, a commitment to take them seriously, and a group declaration to seek resolution makes it easier to do so.

There is a misconception that when we're involved in working groups we're supposed to leave our personal selves at home. But we are still humans, impacted by what others do and say. Lingering resentments interfere with success. Take them seriously and provide positive opportunities for resolving them. I stress this here because this is an area that often undermines groups.

Principle 6: Renewal Requires Openness to New Ideas

The status quo can be powerful, so new ideas need a place to land where they will be given the attention they deserve. Your group needs to develop the habit of encouraging open inquiry and consideration of new ideas. Not doing this can be very costly; again and again, I have seen newcomers become disillusioned and give up as their fresh ideas fall on deaf ears. A process for exploring and vetting ideas is fundamental to a learning organization. It helps you adapt and evolve, which is increasingly important in times of rapid and dramatic change.

Principle 7: Renewal Requires Planning for the Future

Groups need to know where they're going and how they'll get there. Clear plans for the future are essential for achieving the synergy of everyone's combined efforts.

An example is strategic planning. This is a renewal practice because it involves review of what has happened, where the group is at present, an assessment of the environment, and a declaration of where the group is headed and how it plans to get there. The process of planning connects individuals to the same path.

Succession planning—determining what will happen when leadership changes—is equally important. Without it, uncertainty distracts the group from its potential. This is particularly critical in founder-led organizations that tend to be founder-centric. What will happen when this person retires, or when they decide to move on to another endeavor? Ultimately this is about maintaining the integrity of the group so that it survives irrespective of any particular members.

Principle 8: Renewal Must Address Transitions

Times of transition are especially important in groups and call for special attention. These may be times of substantial organizational change, such as reorganization, beginning or ending new programs or initiatives, or changes in upper-level leadership.

While such flux can be unsettling, it contains opportunities for renewal. When someone leaves or enters the group or changes status within it, the group's identity and culture are affected and new possibilities are created.

All of these times of transition call for a renewal process so that the group can *con-*

sciously reconstitute itself in terms of its values and vision in order to maintain integrity and momentum.

Seeing a Breakdown as a Matter of Renewal

A small-business client of mine had begun subcontracting some of his work to a technician at an outside lab. He was initially disappointed in the quality of the service but immediately saw this dilemma as a matter of renewal. He realized that in order to get the level of quality he wanted, he needed to take responsibility for bringing everyone, including outside contractors, into his way of doing things. By taking time to share his inspiration and clarify agreements, he was able to bring this technician into the culture of his business. Now they have a very profitable relationship.

Principle 9: It's Not Just What You Do, but How You Do It

Developing your intentional renewal practice is also about looking at *how* you do what you're already doing. This means asking questions like these: Do we have an employee awards program that doesn't really inspire anyone? Did we create a strategic plan that doesn't actually drive what we do on a day-to-day basis? Do our meetings drag on and fail to energize everyone? Are we creating the results we said we would? Are we treating each other the way we said we would?

This isn't about becoming so self-conscious that you can never act because you have to analyze everything first. On the contrary, renewal practice means you will dedicate times for these activities of review, assessment, and revision. Then you can relax and take care of business, knowing that you're working in the best way to achieve your goals and that you have a sound process to ensure this remains the case.

Principle 10: Renewal Requires a Time Commitment

It's easy to overlook or push aside the commitment of time that renewal requires. It's tempting to consider it a luxury you cannot afford because the needs surrounding you seem more pressing. You might categorize renewal practice as a good thing, something you might get to tomorrow—only to find that tomorrow never arrives. This is short-sighted and wastes the group's potential.

Establishing agreed-upon routines for renewal allows people to relax, confident that there is a time and place for concerns and new ideas to be considered. For instance, if I know that I can bring up a concern about a broken agreement at our routine staff meeting (or other renewal event), I'm less likely to react out of anger while in the midst of a project deadline.

Practices for Renewal

Now that you have the fundamental principles of renewal practice under your belt, let's examine some practices that will build the renewal element of group alchemy into your organization, enabling you to refresh and reinvigorate your work.

Make a Commitment to Renewal

The first step is to make a *group agreement to practice renewal* and to *devise an action plan* based on your assessment of valuable opportunities for positive renewal. This should include an annual renewal event where you can engage in a comprehensive review of your performance, agreements, and commitments and make a plan for any changes you find are needed. Be sure to focus on the *internal functioning of the group* in addition to its external performance.

Conduct a Renewal Assessment

A renewal assessment gives you information about whether you have sufficient renewal practices in place. This means looking at small, incidental moments as well as substantial, orchestrated events for the ways in which you are currently renewing your group, determining whether these forms of renewal serve your commitments, and installing conscious practices that foster growth, improvement, and adaptation. Possible tools to use include surveys, a climate assessment, interviews, group exercises, and discussions.

Such an assessment addresses questions such as these: Are we still committed to our inspiration? Are we in integrity with how we define our mission or have we drifted from it? Are the elements of group alchemy present and optimized? (You can use the assessment questions in the appendix to help you evaluate this.) Are there any unresolved differences in perspective, disagreements, or issues of procedure that need to be resolved? Are we in integrity with our agreements? Do we need any new agreements? Are we getting the results we said we would? What do we need to change about how we work in order to improve our results? Do we have practices that help the group adjust and redefine itself during times of transition such as organizational change or changes in personnel as people leave or join the group? What can we celebrate about what we are doing and how we're doing it?

Create Structure for Renewal

Like all other elements of group alchemy, renewal needs a structure to ensure that it becomes part of the culture. This gives everyone assurance that there are ways to deal with things that need adjustment or revision; people know they won't be stuck for long.

Having a routine structure for renewal makes it easier to broach uncomfortable issues; these don't have to wait for an individual to break into the workflow and start the conversation. A pre-agreed process for renewal can also allow some things to ride; you know there will be a formal opportunity to deal with them later—after the deadline, or at the next staff meeting, or during the annual review. Here are some suggestions for creating such a structure.

- Make sure your calendar is full of renewal practices. Small, routine practices such as having a time set aside in meetings can help you deal with day-to-day issues and integrate new knowledge and experiences quickly. Larger and periodic events such as an annual retreat provide for going into more depth and getting fresh perspectives.

- Get creative and design your process together so all of you can define what really works for your group. Management cannot decide on its own which practices are renewing. One group might prefer a formal year-end meeting while another might prefer having a committee write up a report and then have it acted out in a playful get-together that includes skits.

- Make reviewing your renewal practice part of your renewal practice. This can be as simple as a quick check-in at a regular meeting; it can also be part of your annual assessment process. This will ensure that your renewal practice doesn't grow stale.

- Decide on the things you want to do in each of the principles of renewal. Consider ordinary activities as well as special events that might you do weekly, monthly, quarterly, or annually.

You might have already created some of these structures as you worked in each previous element. A useful step is to collate them into a calendar and add any additional options you can think of. People with differing proclivities and experiences may be naturally attentive to particular elements of success and can provide leadership in those elements. You can download a worksheet to help with collating and summarizing your renewal activities on my website at www.groupalchemy.net/renewal_plan.

Here are some examples of renewal activities:

- A weekly check-in at staff meetings to acknowledge what is going well

- A special periodic "spring cleaning" event that gives everyone a chance to bring forward anything that they think is not working

- A strategic planning process

- Orientation sessions for new members

- Exit interviews for members leaving the group

Create Renewal Agreements

Create any agreements you need that will support your renewal process. This might include a calendar of activities, leaders for those activities, and ways to assess their effectiveness.

Maintain Your Practices in Each of the Other Elements

Remember the interrelated nature of all the elements of group alchemy. The structures you created in each element are part of renewing your group. For example, when groups in my workshops create their renewal action plan, they inevitably identify things in each of the other elements that they consider key to their renewal.

Renewal: Lessons Learned

Success is not a destination. It's a continuing journey.
—Mark Laret

We have established that renewal is a natural cultural process that occurs as a result of everything we do. But as an element of group alchemy, renewal refers to the *set of conscious practices* you can use to refresh your commitments, reaffirm what works, and change what doesn't.

When we are not alert to the creative power of what we say and do, we often create results that contradict what we say we want. The failure to understand this aspect of culture is a major reason why groups are not as powerful as they might be. They have a huge reservoir of potential sitting untapped. Renewal practices will help you avoid that fate.

Keeping groups aligned around inspiration and effectively combining talents and perspectives require attention and intention. Without attending to what keeps the vision alive, most groups degenerate over time. Nothing lasts without nourishment. So it is with group effectiveness. Don't take it for granted. You have to take responsibility for continuity and deliberately attend to the future.

Practicing renewal consciously and consistently—even when things are going well—keeps you in good shape to handle times of sudden change or upheaval. When you regularly assess how you're doing and address opportunities for improvement by drawing on the full talent available in your group, you can more easily do the same when things get tough.

Mastering What Works

Routinely clarifying what's working and what isn't, through strong renewal practices, gives you the opportunity to identify the skills you need to continue creating what works—and *master* those skills. Developing mastery is the sixth and final element of the group alchemy formula.

Resources

For Assessment:

Appreciative Inquiry. The AI Commons is a worldwide portal devoted to the fullest sharing of academic resources and practical tools on Appreciative Inquiry and the rapidly growing discipline of positive change. http://appreciativeinquiry.case.edu/

Appreciative Inquiry is a methodology used by groups to cooperatively explore what is working well in an organization, so they may plan and implement further positive action. This process encourages change in other areas of the organization that may not be functioning as well. The AI method inspires mutual imagination, innovation, and creative thinking, promoting positive action to side-step habitual obstacles and ineffective ways of thinking about challenging issues.

The Foundation Center Toolkit for Assessing Social Impact

http://trasi.foundationcenter.org/browse_toolkit.php

Organizational Surveys: Tools for Assessment and Change, Allen I. Kraut, Jossey-Bass, 1996.

For Sparking Creativity:

Imagine, Jonah Lehrer, Houghton Mifflin Harcourt, 2012.

Making Ideas Happen: Overcoming the Obstacles Between Vision and Reality, Scott Belsky, Penguin Group, 2010.

The Power of Full Engagement: Managing Energy, Not Time, is the Key to High Performance and Personal Renewal, Jim Loehr and Tony Schwartz, Free Press, 2003.

For Planning:

Strategic Planning for Public and Nonprofit Organizations: A Guide to Strengthening and Sustaining Organizational Achievement, John M. Bryson, Jossey Bass, 2011.

Simplified Strategic Planning: The No-Nonsense Guide for Busy People Who Want Results Fast, Robert Bradford, J. Peter Duncan, Brian Tarcy, and Robert W. Bradford, Chandler House, 1999.

Team-Based Strategic Planning: A Complete Guide to Structuring, Facilitating, and Implementing the Process, C. Davis Fogg, Createspace, 2010.

Element Six:

Mastery

Improve performance

Stoke the fires of success

Expand possibilities

Get on the path of mastery and stay on it. Over the long haul,
there's nothing like the path of mastery to lead you to an energetic life.
—George Leonard

This book has now provided you with the essential elements you need to create your culture of success. You have the unity of shared purpose that comes from clearly defined *inspiration*. Your *agreements* and *accountability* practices provide the necessary structure for collaboration. And your habits of *acknowledgment* and *renewal* provide reinforcement and feedback about what is working and what needs to change in order to improve results.

Now you can focus on how to continue to strengthen all of these elements of group alchemy and develop the additional skills you need to create the quality of collaboration that will take you where you want to go. This requires ongoing exploration and learning. We see this in every endeavor that values excellence, even transcendence: sports, the arts, professions, trades, spiritual life—and outstanding leadership and groups.

Enthusiasm for learning and commitment to developing new skills form the mindset of *mastery*. When your commitment is structured to provide routine and systematic opportunities for learning high-level skills of collaboration, you establish a standard for excellence in your group culture. The result is increased confidence and vigor within the group that feeds your inspiration, supports your agreements, and encourages accountability. Now there are *no limits* to the quality of success you can achieve.

This chapter shows you how to structure your group's ongoing learning and development by explaining the key areas that are essential to mastering collaboration, methods you can use to pursue your development, and the practices that will help you establish a culture of learning that supports continuous improvement.

The mastery task of powerful groups is to create
ongoing opportunities for members to improve their
personal performance and develop proficiency in group effectiveness.

Learning the Skill of Group

Collaboration needs to be learned. It's an art, really, that is based on a
few powerful principles. Most people aren't familiar with those principles.
They've never been taught them.
—David Straus, *How to Make Collaboration Work*

Most people come into groups hoping for the best—that everyone will work well together and great things will happen. And sometimes this happy scenario actually occurs. But as we know, it doesn't always. People don't automatically fall into easy harmony. Different viewpoints and styles of working collide and result in frustration if not outright conflict. Such tension can be subtle or overt, but results *always* suffer when people don't know what to do about it.

The simple fact is that the skills and awareness required to set the stage for powerful collaboration do not come naturally. They must be learned—and most of us have not had sufficient opportunities to do so.

The art of collaboration depends on opportunities to gain deep knowledge of your own and others' strengths. Then, it requires learning practical techniques that aid in integrating different approaches, styles, talents, backgrounds, and perspectives into optimal methods of group problem solving and decision making. The cause of excellent group results is further promoted by learning new ways to increase your own personal performance, negotiation skills, and emotional skills.

We will explore these crucial elements of mastery further in this chapter. For now, let's take a closer look at the kinds of challenges we face in our groups today that call for continuous learning.

The Multicultural Dimension

At the beginning of the book we touched on the implications of diverse backgrounds in terms of our ability to work in concert. We all grew up with a set of notions, learned in our families and communities, about what's right and how life works. From these same sources we acquired an "operating system" of social strategies for getting along and getting things done. This means that what each of us believe is "right" and what we understand about how things work are "local knowledge," specific to our particular backgrounds.

Like all operating systems, this set of notions about what we can expect from others and how we should behave runs in the background, usually beneath our awareness. We bring these styles and strategies to the groups we join and proceed from these assumptions: "I know how to get along. Everyone else knows what I know and sees it the way I see it. Now let's just get on with our work."

When everyone is situated in the same cultural viewpoint, that approach can be efficient. We don't have to second-guess our actions all the time. But as we discussed in the chapter on agreements, very often such assumptions don't work at all.

Most of the groups we work in these days are increasingly "illocal," to coin a phrase, meaning that they are made up of people from different places and backgrounds; differing experiential bases have been tossed together. These include family, education, profession, gender, ethnicity, and life history.

The result is that our individual repertoires of group skills can vary tremendously. People are working from different operating systems. Sprinkle this spice mix of diversity on top of differences in personalities and it's a lot to contend with. Simply put, in these situations there are a lot of competing ideas for how to make things work. This can have dramatic effects as people work together to solve problems and make decisions.

Hurry Up! Wait!

Tania prefers to hash out problems by taking lots of time to describe the situation and analyze its causes. Meanwhile Nadia prefers to experiment with ideas—to get on with it and try something to see if it will work. Listening to them speak in turn, you'd think they were having two different conversations. Their discussions often leave Tania feeling rushed and anxious, concerned that important information is being overlooked, while Nadia tends to feel bogged down by Tania's approach. It's easy to see how judgments such as "rash" and "impetuous" and "obsessive" and "fearful" can become ingrained in a relationship like this. In group meetings where the two are present, tension clouds the proceedings. Loss of effectiveness and hard feelings ensue simply because people are not aware of the true value of each approach in achieving high-quality results, and no one knows how to integrate them.

In addition to having colliding styles, such as those of Tania and Nadia, people may be under a lot of pressure to perform and shoulder much responsibility. You now have a

Becoming "Wise Ones"

You might recall that this reliance on assumptions is intrinsically human. It worked for our ancestors, and we inherited this way of being. We rely on assumptions millions of times every day as we successfully navigate our lives: from the practical matters of how to conduct a transaction with the clerk in the grocery store to how to engage with our coworkers for the project we're working on. We trust our knowledge about the world, and for good reason.

When those assumptions lead us into difficulty we rely on another intrinsically human trait. While we might not have inherited all of the particular skills we need to participate effectively in our groups today, we did inherit from our ancestors the capacity to learn: to become aware of the things we're doing and intentionally change our behavior. This capacity to learn and change is what makes us the "wise ones"—if we are to live up to our name Homo sapiens—and when it comes to groups, it's our saving grace.

web of very complicated needs and motivations. Then throw in rapid change, and it's no wonder that the path to productive and satisfying groups can seem mysterious. Why would we ever expect that we could come together and automatically know how to work together? Isn't it remarkable that things work as well as they do?

Unless we pursue learning in the area of group functioning, we are in effect running an operating system that's sorely out of date. We're acting on assumptions about how things should work that just do not hold up.

Groups made up of complex sets of relationships between diverse members simply demand conscious behavior and high-level skills in collaboration. If we want a creative flow of ideas and efficient coordination, we need more than the push-pull of the default modes of solo operators. The answer lies in learning new ways to work.

Mastery in personal and group performance skills can create the amalgamation of abilities that generates remarkable results. Let's look more closely at the particular ways in which developing mastery does this.

Reflection Questions

1. Are you learning and practicing new skills in your job and in the group?

2. Are you personally committed to excellence in group-building behaviors? Is your group committed to increasing its performance?

3. Is your group characterized by much interpersonal frustration and conflict?

4. Do you process disagreements in a constructive way that enhances learning?

5. Are people defensive about their positions, or are they willing to change their positions based on new ideas?

6. Do group members openly admit and discuss their mistakes and difficulties as a way to further learn in the group?

The Alchemy of Mastery

New ideas create options. They make it possible to get free of the autopilot of the past: the limiting beliefs, unproductive habits, and default social patterns that easily develop in groups. Consistent practices that apply new perspectives build mastery and generate these effects:

Ease and Efficiency

When differences are understood and valued, they can be worked with in a complementary way to create results that would not be possible without the contribution of those different perspectives and skills. The group can stop wasting time on unproductive distractions and arguments that tend to develop in situations such Tania and Nadia's where a lot of creative potential is lost in confusion and competition.

As people learn about these differences in personal styles in all the stages of learning and problem solving while developing strong group collaboration skills, they can engage in an efficient process that draws on everyone's strengths without being distracted by what used to appear as lack of cooperation or stubbornness.

Flexibility and Adaptability

Having more options—in thinking and behavior—creates greater flexibility. Empowered with better information and a bigger picture, we can make conscious choices to do what works best in the current situation.

Continuing with the example of Nadia and Tania's different strengths in problem solving, once I understand that each stance represents a strength for the group, I can stop insisting on my point of view and listen to others with an appreciation that they can see things I might not. And when I also know that others appreciate the contributions of my distinct perspective, I can be less concerned with being right, or being heard, and can engage at the appropriate times with helpful additions to the process.

This kind of cooperativeness and deep listening generates the learning that is needed to quickly adapt to changes in the environment. As we have already discussed in the renewal element, such adaptability is the key to sustained success.

Creativity and Innovation

New ideas depend on new perspectives. If the group is skilled in listening to and incorporating diversity, it can reap the benefits of differing backgrounds and experiences. Then diverse viewpoints and talents can be brought to bear to fully address each stage of the cycle of learning and problem solving. This is the synergy that sparks creativity.

Furthermore, by making the commitment to learning that is at the heart of mastery—and with a solid practice in agreements and accountability—you can support and encourage calculated risk-taking. You can see mistakes as learning opportunities instead of failures; this is at the heart of innovation.

The Organization Learns

Organizational learning is widely understood to be a key to continued success. This begins with individuals and proceeds through the group when it puts in place structures and routines for learning new skills. When these are part of the organization's culture through a committed mastery practice, the group can regularly transcend its previous level of performance and respond to new possibilities.

Inspiration Is Refreshed and Renewed

Learning activities create experiences of expanded possibility and accomplishment that feed inspiration. As this occurs in individuals, it also becomes true for the group and becomes part of the culture. My clients routinely name professional learning and development experiences in the list of things they plan to do to increase their inspiration.

Personal Fulfillment Increases

This benefit is twofold. First, as the entire group becomes more skilled in listening and incorporating new ideas and perspectives, people are supported in fully participating in the group and bringing all of their talents to bear. The result is a substantial increase in satisfaction and connectedness.

Secondly, opportunities to learn help meet people's fundamental desires for growth. The frequency with which my clients identify learning and professional development opportunities as important tells me how highly we all value these in terms of personal fulfillment.

The Cost When Mastery Is Weak

Old beliefs do not lead to new cheese.
—Spencer Johnson

We all know that almost everyone can tell stories about challenges or frustrating experiences they have faced while working in groups. Many of these are the result of differences in backgrounds, styles, and perspectives among people that we've been discussing in this chapter. When the nature of these frustrations goes unrecognized and unresolved, they can lead to conflict and even the complete disintegration of the group.

Lack of knowledge about diversity and personal styles often means the group has a low tolerance for them, and this can lead to *frustration and conflict* as people approach situations differently; those differences are often interpreted as uncooperativeness, stubbornness, or obstinacy. Resentment and contempt build, undermining the trust and openness needed for creativity and success.

Lack of skills in group process, from facilitating meetings to leading a problem-solving effort, results in poor utilization of people's time and talents. This is why groups that do not strive for mastery experience *wasted time and low productivity*.

Having few options for getting "unstuck" from limiting patterns of behavior means that people act using whatever resources they brought to the group. If these are weak, there is no leverage for growth or making improvements, personally or as a group. The group suffers *low achievement*.

When group members lack awareness of their styles and patterns, individuals often engage in unconscious behaviors and operate out of fear and the need for control. Those fear-based patterns usually result in *power struggles* as people strive to influence the group's course and protect themselves and their territory. Power struggles overwhelm accomplishments.

Conflicts and power struggles are usually accompanied by feelings of being disrespected and disregarded. People don't believe they can fully participate or contribute their best ideas. Disappointment and frustration set in and lead to withdrawal. The group suffers from *stagnation and a loss of creativity*.

As the lack of knowledge about how to develop talents and work with differences leads to frustration, a general sense among group members of apathy—or worse —toward one another leads to ugly personal conflicts. The group loses what cohesion it had as people retreat into cliques or isolation. It develops a *negative culture* characterized by cynicism, complaining, gossip, backbiting, and even sabotage. Talented and inspired people who have other options choose to leave. Ultimately, the group cannot sustain itself and *disintegrates*.

Principles of Mastery Practice

Clearly, without learning and development as an essential part of its culture, your group's future will not be bright. But it's not at all difficult to put your group on a path of expansion and improvement. The following principles of practice will guide you.

Principle 1: Mastery Is a Cycle of Illumination and Practice

It's what you learn after you think you know it all that really counts.
—John Wooden

Learning gives you options. You don't have to remain stuck doing the same thing and hoping for a different result. You can change to better serve your intentions. You can think of this in terms of mastering a craft; the more you practice, the more skilled you become—*and* there is no end point where you have "arrived." There is always the opportunity to get even better at group work than you are today, becoming ever more conscious and intentional in the elements of inspiration, agreement, accountability, acknowledgment, and renewal; achieving *mastery* in the art and science of collaboration.

Principle 2: Mastery Occurs in Four Domains

The areas of learning and development that are vital to group effectiveness can be organized into four domains. Each is an area that can be plumbed at some depth, and I can't cover them exhaustively here, but I will I briefly describe each. At the end of the chapter I offer further suggestions for exploration and practice that I believe are especially helpful.

I encourage you to create habits of learning in each of these domains, and I hope you will enjoy discovering the resources that work for you as your inclinations, needs, and interests direct you. I would love to hear from you about the things you find most helpful.

As you review these domains, consider your own group as you consider the following questions: What standard of excellence is your group committed to? What development opportunities do you provide for your members in service of that standard of excellence?

Mastery in Job Performance

Improving the skills needed to perform necessary tasks is essential to success. This is widely recognized because it directly impacts the outcomes organizations most often measure. Because this domain is inherently job, industry, and organization specific, I leave it to you to decide how best to include this domain in your mastery practice and establish meaningful learning opportunities for your group members. This domain addresses the question: *What skills do I need to perform my job to the best level possible?*

Mastery in Personal Effectiveness

To improve the team, improve yourself.
—John C. Maxwell

Mastery in personal effectiveness means improving your personal capabilities to fully contribute to the group's success while also achieving your personal goals. Advancing in this domain entails developing emotional intelligence, expanding skills in constructive communication, improving adeptness in working with conflict, and optimizing personal performance. It all begins with keen awareness of your own personal traits, skills, talents, predispositions, and preferences. Then you can develop the skills identified by asking this question: *What contribution am I making to the group and how might I improve?*

Formal Leadership
The way you model the value of diversity and personal flexibility can have a dramatic influence on the group that encourages others to do the same. This can be a challenge because we typically reward constancy in leadership. But the ability to learn and change will reward you personally with more successful groups and offer an invaluable inducement to others.

Mastery in Diversity

It is how we handle ourselves in our relationships that determines how well we do once we are in a given job.
—Daniel Goleman, *Emotional Intelligence*

As we've discussed, people's talents, skills, and preferences vary according to their innate characteristics and personal backgrounds. I construe diversity very broadly to include personality; life experiences such as education, profession, ethnicity, race, gender, and age; and geographic and life histories. Skills in integrating those diverse talents give the group a distinctive advantage. This domain addresses the question: *What unique contributions do others bring to the group and how might I better recognize and work with those talents?*

Mastery in Group Culture and Process

While mastery on an individual level is crucial for group success, an individual can only take it so far. The next level of success is realized when a group works *together* to learn about the special dynamics that operate in groups and what to do to elevate the group's functioning. This means attending to the interpersonal nature of the work and focusing on *shared practices:* the behaviors and interactions that foster successful collaboration.

Clearly, I view this formula for group alchemy as the basis for developing mastery in this domain. The understanding of culture, leadership, and personality in groups and the practices you have developed here will help you thrive as a group.

Informal Leadership
This is another area where any individual member of the group can contribute greatly to the quality of how the group works. Taking charge of your own future and stepping onto the path of mastery can inspire others to do so as well. Any knowledge you share will help others, and changes in your own behavior as you apply your learning can have substantial effects across the group.

In addition to the cultural practices we have developed here, the *process* a group uses to do its work can substantially determine the quality of the outcome. Good intentions and smart, knowledgeable people are not enough. There has to be a methodology for bringing together the ideas and perspectives of the group in a systematic way if the full potential of the group is to be realized.

This means developing group process skills in problem solving, decision making, effective meeting strategies, and facilitation. Here is where you address the question: *What can I/we do that will improve our ability to combine our talents more effectively?*

Principle 3: Mastery Takes Place in Individuals

> *Individual learning is at the heart of organizational learning—organizations learn through individuals. You cannot improve how the organization functions without individuals improving the way they perform their roles in the organization.*
> —Shoji Shiba and David Walden

Because groups are made up of individuals, the success of the group is dependent upon each individual embracing the learning challenge and building their own awareness of self and as a member of the group.

Principle 4: Mastery Takes Place in the Group

While some learning must happen at the individual level, certain learning can only happen as a *group experience*. This includes insight into the makeup of your particular group and how the universal principles of group effectiveness will work within it.

Exploration within the group also provides a language for talking about the group's potential as well as the challenges its diversity presents. Doing this provides openness and a shared language that makes it easier to address any troublesome situations that might arise in the future. I've witnessed some profound "light bulb moments" and inspiring conversations as groups explore what it means to recognize the differences in each other's talents and styles and how to connect them productively instead of being frustrated by them.

Principle 5: Mastery Is for Everyone

Mastery is not merely the purview of the manager or supervisor of the group, or of the most interested members, but is the work of all members so that *everyone can take full responsibility for the group enterprise*.

We know that each member has substantial direct and indirect effects on the group as a whole. In his book *Teamwork Is an Individual Skill*, Christopher Avery emphasizes that teams perform to the level of their least committed member. A lack of commitment to mastery means that you are limited by the one with the most restricted repertoire of collaborative behaviors, and your results will suffer. When I discussed this issue with a musician friend once, she told me, "Oh yes, musicians always say it doesn't matter how good you are or how much you practice. If your drummer (or bass player, or lead guitar, etc.) isn't good—then you're no good."

> **Culture Note**
> This is another valuable place to check your "ideal" culture versus your "real" one. For example, do you say that you want to be the best at what you do? Look to see whether you provide the structure for achieving this. Do you make it easy for group members to learn? Do you provide time and opportunity for the group to work together on creating the habits of success? Then you will be in a position to create those learning opportunities that support your ideals.

The fact is that we all can benefit from learning how to improve our ability to engage constructively in relationships. Make it part of your culture—part of what it means to belong in your group with the associated rewards and acknowledgment. The practice section in this chapter as well as the rest of the group alchemy elements will help you to do that.

Principle 6: Mastery Includes Learning from Experts

There is a tremendous amount of available knowledge and expertise about how to achieve highly successful groups, based on many decades of sophisticated research. I urge you to draw upon it. You don't have to reinvent this wheel; you only need to adapt it to your situation.

This can come from reading books, attending workshops, bringing in a consultant to work with your group, or participating in webinars. New media for learning are being developed every year. Draw on the media that work for you so that you can make learning opportunities frequent and accessible.

Principle 7: Mastery Includes Learning from Each Other in Your Group

Some of the most transformational learning that powerful groups experience comes from the things the members share with each other about their insights and experiences.

Taking time frequently (even short moments during meetings, for instance) to reflect as a group and discuss your experiences means you can build deep learning into your routine. Learning can also happen through special workshops and retreats. Creating these opportunities is part of making mastery a genuine aspect of your culture.

Now that we have outlined the key principles for how to build your mastery practice, we can look further at the practices that will enable you to develop mastery as a routine and integral part of your culture.

Practices to Build Mastery

If people knew how hard I worked to get my mastery,
it wouldn't seem so wonderful at all.
—Michelangelo

Mastery, by definition, means having a practice. The following steps will help you build an effective, intentional learning practice in your group.

Make a Commitment to Mastery

You know what making a commitment in your group looks like now; apply all of the group alchemy elements to make a group declaration of your commitment to learning with the requisite agreements that will support it. This includes fully engaging the learning process in the group and a commitment of leadership to provide the appropriate time and resources for those opportunities. Group transformation begins the moment you declare such a commitment.

Conduct a Mastery Assessment

Mastery begins with assessing your current situation. I encourage the use of strength-based tools and methods of appreciative inquiry. Both guide an assessment from a focus on strengths rather than problems—akin to the mind-set of possibility that I encouraged in the inspiration element. Then you can answer the question, *What more do we need to know about what works in groups to achieve our goals?* And you will be able to identify where gains in effectiveness can be achieved most quickly.

You can conduct a survey or hold an open discussion that helps you assess your overall organizational climate. Review the assessment work you have done in each of the other elements of this formula for group alchemy to see where you might want to provide learning opportunities.

If the group has a history that seems to be weighing it down, does that history include disappointment, resignation, cynicism, or notions of "Well, this is how it is—nothing ever changes"? If it does, these all need to be expressed and acknowledged. Give the group an opportunity to explore their collective feelings and attitudes so you can resolve old issues. This will allow you to create from the present, working with a view of what is possible.

Be sure to openly discuss the results of group assessments. The point in mastery practice is for the group to learn about itself, so any assessment results must be available to everyone in it.

Here are some assessment questions you might investigate with your group:

1. Do members of your group seek out knowledge of group dynamics and practices that support success, or does group effectiveness seem mysterious?

2. Do people explore differences in personal styles and work to integrate them so as to expand the effectiveness of the group?

3. Do you use problem-solving models that encourage and facilitate working with differing points of view?

4. Do you make decisions efficiently and with appropriate levels of input?

5. Do you have routine ways to develop new skills and deepen awareness about the group?

6. Do you inspire and acknowledge each other for personal excellence in job performance and in the group's process? Do you provide structures and foster habits that encourage, support, and reward learning?

Review Your Inspiration

Review the statements and conversations you have concerning your inspiration, the stories that define you. Consider where you need new skills and knowledge in support of your mission. The more closely you connect your learning and development opportunities with what motivates your group, the more successful you will be.

Create a Structure to Support Mastery

I have stressed the need for structure throughout this book. In fact, the entire formula is a structure for creating and maintaining practices and habits that work. This is one of the crucial lessons of mastery. So of course the practice of mastery needs structure to keep it active in the group over time and through whatever challenges may arise. This is what will serve to inspire continuing growth and help keep you going through the learning plateaus, pitfalls, and challenges that can cause many people to give up or settle for so-so performance when they're stretching to hone new skills.

Some possibilities for structure include:

•   Build it into your calendar.

•   You can hold special learning events like a workshop or retreat.

•   I strongly recommend short, simple activities you can do frequently and include in other things you do routinely, such as short check-ins, discussions of new ideas or learnings, or surveys. For instance, you can set aside time (ten minutes or so) at each regular staff meeting, or have a brown-bag lunch once a month dedicated to a learning experience. This can be an exercise the group does together, or a lightning round to share good reads, new ideas, or any new things individuals have tried lately. You could include things outside normal work and task areas when you do this because learning often comes from endeavors that are unrelated to a given task—in other dimensions of life.

- Create opportunities for people to share their independent learning with the group. For example, have a special five-minute "quick share" in your meetings where anyone can relate something they have learned or tried and how it worked to improve a situation.

- Conduct periodic assessments to discover where learning opportunities would be beneficial. For more discussion on this, see the chapter on the renewal element.

- Appoint a leader for each group alchemy element who can provide leadership for promoting and encouraging development activities in that element. Rotate this position to help everyone develop their mastery in each element.

- Use the group alchemy formula to structure meetings and events. This means making sure that your agenda or format includes some sort of practice in each element. For example, your regular staff meeting can open with an inspiring story that speaks to your mission. You then create intentional agreements as they relate to your discussions and decisions, or quickly review the agreements you have in place for conducting meetings—and use them. Include an accountability review on any items from your last meeting. You can practice acknowledgment as you address various topics, or during a special moment at the end of the meeting, or both. Then as a part of your renewal practice you can do a quick assessment of the meeting to affirm what worked and revise what didn't in your next meeting.

- Using the formula to structure your work means that you're continually building skills and developing mastery in maintaining the elements of alchemy, always building your conscious culture. And you'll be getting great results!

- Appoint someone as your process leader, who can give special attention to your group process. You can think of this person as serving as an internal consultant who is focused on *how* you're working as a group to help you get to the best results. This means their attention is on questions such as, are you using the group alchemy practices in each element? Are you using the problem-solving and decision-making methods you have adopted? Do you conduct your meetings with effective process modalities? You can rotate this function periodically so everyone with the skill and inclination to focus some of their attention on the group's effectiveness can make their contribution.

- Provide meaningful acknowledgment and rewards to individuals and the group for pursuing mastery. When you provide the time, acknowledgment, and financial incentives that encourage learning and development, you make it part of your culture. It might be helpful to review the chapter on acknowledgement as you work on this.

- Have the group brainstorm ideas for structuring your learning. Be creative.

- Do what works for your group. There is no right or wrong way to structure your continued learning and skill building. If your group is a very intellectual one, bringing in literature could be helpful. Just be sure to move into a practice and experimentation exercise too. If your group is very kinesthetic, you might start with exercises and experiences, as long as you spend time reflecting and developing conceptual understanding as well. All of these styles are important for all groups—and you can always start with the access point that is most comfortable for your group. If your group has very diverse preferences, vary your approach to keep it fresh. Just be sure to remind people that you will get back to their preferred approach to learning repeatedly.

- Practice renewal and include reviewing and refreshing your mastery practices.

Mastery: Lessons Learned

> *If you always do what you always did, you will always get what you always got.*
> —Mark Twain

You don't have to do what you've always done. You can expand your knowledge beyond what you know today and develop new ways of doing things—and get better outcomes.

A fundamental principle of the group alchemy approach is that moving to greater consciousness and intention improves all relationships and their capacity to produce results. This is how you skillfully draw all your talents and wisdom together to create the world you envision.

The resilience and responsiveness that today's world requires just magnifies the need for proficiency in powerful methods for working with differences. All relationships involve reconciliation of differences: of perspectives, preferences, needs, and desires. We cannot leave talents latent, needs suppressed, or conflict unaddressed if we want outstanding success.

The fact is that we all can benefit from learning how to improve our ability to engage constructively in relationships. Avoiding the silent truces, resignation, and withholding that characterize many groups requires taking the journey of mastery—mastery of self and group—together.

The result is that you have confidence that your group is working at its optimum—or at least you are always seeking that aim, together. You can be confident that the solutions you devise collectively will be superior to anything any ordinary group, can do. You can count on collective commitment to those solutions, and surety of their success. You will experience better-quality relationships with less stress, conflict, and disruptive frustration. More enjoyment will be available to you. When you are developing mastery you can depend on doing better tomorrow than you did today.

Resources

I have included a longer than usual list of resources for this chapter since it's all about learning across multiple domains. This is still just a list to get you started. Have fun exploring!

Personal Effectiveness:

Teamwork Is an Individual Skill, Christopher M. Avery, Berrett-Koehler Publishers, San Francisco, 2001.

Emotional Intelligence, Daniel Goleman, Bantam Books, 2006.

Brain Rules, John Medina, Pear Press, 2008.

Heart Math, a set of scientifically validated tools and techniques that can help people of all ages renew energy, gain greater mental and emotional balance, and build resilience, www.heartmath.org.

Landmark Education, www.landmarkeducation.com.

Communication:

Center for Nonviolent Communication, www.cnvc.org.

Difficult Conversations: How to Discuss What Matters Most, Douglas Stone et al, Penguin Books, 1999.

The Four Conversations: Daily Communication That Gets Results, Jeffrey Ford and Laurie Ford, Berrett-Koehler Publishers, 2009.

Getting Together: Building Relationships As We Negotiate, Roger Fisher and Scott Brown, Penguin Books, 1989.

Ladder of Inference Model. From *The Fifth Discipline Fieldbook*, Peter Senge, Broadway Business, 1994.

That's Not What I Meant!: How Conversational Style Makes or Breaks Relationships, Deborah Tannen, Ballantine, 1986.

Talking from 9 to 5: Women and Men at Work, Deborah Tannen, HarperCollins, 1994.

Diversity:

Embracing Cultural Competency: A Roadmap for Nonprofit Capacity Builders by Patricia St. Onge et al, Fieldstone Alliance with the Alliance for Nonprofit Management, 2009.

Group Effectiveness:

The 17 Indisputable Laws of Teamwork, John C. Maxwell, Thomas Nelson, 2001.

How to Make Collaboration Work, David Straus, Berrett-Koehler Publishers, 2002.

Facilitator's Guide to Participatory Decision-Making, Sam Kaner, et al., Jossey-Bass, San Francisco, 2007.

Four Practical Revolutions in Management: Systems for Creating Unique Organizational Capability, Shoji Shiba and David Walden, Productivity Press, New York, 2001.

The Skilled Facilitator, Roger Schwarz, Josssey-Bass, 2002.

Technology of Participation : Institute for Cultural Affairs, www.ica-usa.org.

Conclusion

Wherever you go, go with all your heart.
—Confucius

By now, as you have adopted the principles and practices in this book, you've probably begun to experience changes in your group. This gives you a preview of what is possible: the more you develop these habits the more you will experience the extraordinary outcomes and positive atmosphere of which your group is capable. You are constructing a whole new way of working together and helping usher in a future that will be more productive, more effective, and eminently more rewarding.

The time and effort you invest in developing new work habits will be returned many times over as your group achieves the efficiencies that group alchemy makes possible. And the more time you spend attending to your processes and habits, the faster you'll get results. Remember that each level of success makes it easier to rise to the next. And there is always a next level. All groups are emergent; their potential continuously expands as their knowledge and experience grow.

As I close, I want to take this opportunity to highlight a few key themes and principles that will help you to continue to get the most out of this work.

Structure, structure, structure.

Throughout this book I have stressed the need for structure to support your best practices. I can't overstate this. *Using* this formula is what makes this method different from an inspiring workshop or a fun teambuilding event. You now have a structure to follow to make sure you continually engage the practices to create lasting change.

We're all working against decades of conditioning within our various cultures: our families, our professions, our institutions, and our society. Adopting the kinds of positive habits discussed in this book, along with periodic check-ins and evaluations, will keep you on track. Admittedly, some of the practices I promote here can be a special challenge for people from particular social and ethnic backgrounds where it's not an inherent part of the culture to be explicit, to make overt requests, or to speak directly to formal authority. But I believe it's necessary for us all to learn to do these things—*especially* in our multicultural world where the potential for misunderstanding is high. A defined structure will help you.

Use the structure you create in this formula during times of trouble.

The structure you put in place when things are going smoothly will reap huge dividends for you when trouble arises. You can review your practices in these elements to identify where your attention will best be placed to address the difficulty at hand.

Change what you are doing when it no longer resonates with the group.

Using the elements as a lens to review your situation can shed light on where you might need to evolve. External circumstances will change, your group will change, and what you need in order to stay productive and efficient may change. Make new agreements when needed. Change your acknowledgment and reward system when appropriate to better respond to your goals. Stay in conversation so you can adapt and your group doesn't become rigid and inflexible.

Be the alchemist in your group.

As you have learned, every person in the group, regardless of formal status or role, influences the nature of the group and the conditions for its success—all the time. This means that *each member of the group can make a difference, right now.*

If you are the group's formal leader, you have a special privilege that allows you to introduce change. But don't fall into the trap of management-centric thinking. The alchemy of success cannot be "installed." It emerges through participation that begins with an invitation.

If you are not the formal leader of your group, you still can express leadership and introduce change. It's common that people see difficulties in terms of what someone else seems to be doing. I often hear about the person who talks too much, or the one who withholds important information, the leader who doesn't provide direction, or the co-worker who is said to have a negative attitude.

But when you take full personal responsibility for the success of your group as well as your own experience, change truly does begin "at home." You don't have to wait for someone else to do something to improve the situation. You might ask for new agreements that will change how the group works. You might spark the group's inspiration by speaking about its vision and goals more often. You could choose to be more communicative and invite others to do the same. Maybe you can bring up a taboo subject that needs to be discussed in service to your mission and to clear the way for more productive activity.

Changing *how you are* in the group and *what you ask from it* will change the group. I've seen it happen again and again: a lone whisper can shift an entire conversation, often in immediate and surprising ways. Raise the question to the group. Spark the conversation. Promote the possibility that you see. Choose inspired action and invite others along.

Your New Normal

> *The future is created one room at a time, one gathering at a time.*
> *Each gathering needs to become an example of the future we want to create.*
> *This means the small group is where transformation takes place.*
> —Peter Block, *Community*

The group alchemy formula is based in a vision of what is possible in groups. It acknowledges that we are all engaged in deeply profound ancient cultural processes and shows you how to enter into them with intention and purpose.

After working with many, many groups I've learned that they contain much wisdom. Trust that. Engage in this process and you will create the conditions for the group's wisdom to more fully emerge and grow. The words my clients use to describe their successful group experiences include *energizing, inspiring, creative, big accomplishments,* and *rewarding.* Now that you have had the opportunity to put some group alchemy tools to work for you, what other words would you use? These qualities and more are right at your fingertips when you commit to a group alchemy practice. It is my heartfelt wish that they become your "new normal."

Enjoy your alchemy. You deserve it.

Appendix A: Assessment Questions

Inspiration

1. Is your group energetic and enthusiastic about what it's doing?

2. Is your group engaged in an inspiration conversation that's reflected in written values, vision, mission, and identity statements?

3. Do your group's members share the same set of core values about their work? Is it evident in the ways people talk and behave?

4. Does everyone share the same vision of what your group is creating? Is the vision significant, clear, and compelling enough to keep the team together?

5. Are you confident that everyone in your group is focused on the same purpose and goals? If each group member were asked to name the top organizational priorities, would the answers be the same?

6. Are people motivated by the part they play in the group's mission? Can each member relate their personal responsibilities to the organization's mission? Do group members help each other find professional fulfillment from the group's work?

7. Do group members refer to its inspiration (vision, values, mission, identity) routinely, especially when making decisions or choosing strategies?

8. Do you hear the group's vision and mission statements reflected in the way people speak?

9. Has the group defined its organizational structure, policies, and procedures to be in line with its inspiration? Are organizational resources—people, time, and money—aligned with the group's stated purpose and goals? Can you clearly see its values expressed throughout all of these areas?

10. Do team members willingly make sacrifices or trade-offs (such as budget, turf, head count) in their departments or areas of expertise for the sake of this mission?

11. Have you hired people who share your values? Do you have a hiring process in place to ensure that new hires understand your vision and mission and see themselves in it? Have you trained people in their jobs in ways that make it possible for them to work in accordance with the group's values? Do you routinely assess your work in terms of your values and mission?

Agreements

1. Can your group identify its structural and behavioral agreements?

2. Does everyone share the same understanding of each other's roles?

3. Are the group's goals explicit agreements, clearly stating what it will do, who will do it, and by when?

4. Are there clear, explicit agreements about *how* you are going to work together as a group?

5. Where are there friction points in your group that might indicate that you need to refine your agreements?

6. Can you identify a time when someone brought up counterproductive behavior in order to establish explicit agreements that support your group's effectiveness?

7. Does your group have an agreement to make and keep agreements? Does it have an agreement to revise agreements as needed?

8. Are there ways to identify any agreements operating in the group that hinder its success?

9. Does everyone in your group make requests when needed in order to resolve a problem or create a more productive environment?

10. Do you employ discussion ground rules so that your meetings are productive and energizing?

11. Do you leave meetings confident that everyone shares the same understanding of decisions reached and that everyone is completely committed to upholding them?

Accountability

1. Do your group's members show that they are willing to accept full responsibility for the consequences of the decisions and actions of the group as a whole?

2. Do you trust your colleagues to deliver on their commitments?

3. Are power plays and manipulation nonexistent (or at least rare)?

4. When things go wrong, do members look to solve the problem rather than avoid it, hide it, or simply find fault?

5. Do members of the group provide honest assessments of each other's work and contributions in the framework of its mission and goals?

6. If someone is not behaving in a manner consistent with your agreements, does someone else in the group raise that issue and call them back to your agreements?

7. Do you have systematic ways of measuring performance and tracking outcomes for individuals and for the group as a whole?

8. Do group members quickly and genuinely own their actions and make amends if they do or say something inappropriate or possibly damaging to an individual or the group as a whole?

Acknowledgment

1. How does the group acknowledge the contributions people make to its most important commitments? Its goals? Its agreements?

2. In what ways do members of the group regularly personally acknowledge each other for the specific ways they contribute to the functioning of the group?

3. How has your group prioritized acknowledgment? How has it made acknowledgment an important part of its leadership practice?

4. Describe how your group's formal structure for acknowledgment links to its values and agreements. Does its reward structure support its values and commitments?

5. Do members of the group feel appreciated and recognized? Is this true across the organization or are there differences between different segments of the organization?

6. In what way does your group's reward structure include developing expertise in group effectiveness?

Renewal

1. Does your group routinely revisit its commitments in inspiration and agreements in order to reaffirm or revise them where needed?

2. Does your group review its process and effectiveness as a group and make any needed adjustments? Do you work to resolve differences in perspective, disagreements, or issues of procedure?

3. Do you routinely assess your results and identify what you need to change about how you work in order to improve your results?

4. Does your group have rituals that reconstitute the group during times of transition, such as organizational change or changes in personnel as people leave or join the group?

5. Is there a process in place for selecting group members that ensures that they share the group's inspiration and are willing to join its agreements?

6. Is there an orientation process in place that helps new members understand and fully own the group's inspiration commitments and agreements?

7. When individual roles change, do you make an intentional effort to clarify these changes for everyone in the work group?

8. Do you frequently celebrate your successes?

Mastery

1. Do you inspire and acknowledge each other for personal excellence in job performance?

2. Does your group have routine ways to develop new skills and deepen awareness about the group?

3. Are there structure and habits for encouraging, supporting, and rewarding learning?

4. Are you personally committed to excellence in group-building behaviors? Is your group committed to increasing its performance?

5. Do people explore differences in personal styles and work to integrate them to expand the group's effectiveness?

6. Does the group use problem-solving models that encourage and facilitate working with differing points of view?

7. Are decisions made efficiently with appropriate levels of input for the particular decision?

8. Does your group process disagreements in a constructive way that enhances learning? Are people defensive about their positions, or are they willing to change their positions based on new ideas?

9. Do group members openly admit and discuss their mistakes and difficulties as a way to further learn in the group?

Appendix B: Domains for Mastery

My purpose with this appendix is to organize what is a large and diverse array of tools for developing mastery and make it easy for you to see how they fit in the overall development of group culture. I break them into three categories, and I leave it to you to explore the personal and professional development and training options that may be available to you in each area, as the spirit moves you.

The chart at the end summarizes the key areas of focus that affect group success. Working in each will improve performance; perhaps the chart will help you identify where your group would benefit most so you can start there.

Mastering Personal Effectiveness involves learning how your life experiences have shaped you and how you might consciously shape yourself going forward. This begins with cultivating self-awareness about who you are and how you affect those around you. The key is to see that you have options and power in every situation to change what doesn't work into something that does. Success means not waiting for someone else to change.

As a personal journey, this can be life changing. When it is engaged in a safe environment within a group where people can be authentic and talk openly about their experiences, the group can also transform in response to the resulting openness, authenticity, and mutual understanding.

The tools used usually involve an assessment or an inventory such as the Myers-Briggs Personality Type. These inventories are typically a series of questions or options that help reveal your preferences or routine behaviors out of a range of possibilities. They often result in a summary description or a profile with names like "Risk-Taker," "Mediator," or "Director."

To get the benefits that these tools offer, I urge you not to get stuck on them as having the truth but to view them as interpretive frameworks—like a pair of glasses that shine light in a particular way and illuminate a new vantage point that's not always visible in your everyday experience. Then you can determine what is personally meaningful and useful and how that information can help you develop effective ways to achieve your intentions and goals.

The items listed on the chart point to areas for development. Resources are widely available in all of these areas.

Mastering Diversity is based on something we all know but easily forget: the way we are is not the way everyone is. The tools and exercises that help you identify your own style in developing own personal effectiveness also teach you about the range of possible styles that others might possess.

This means that learning about your personal style is also a valuable way to learn about human diversity in all its forms, from culture and ethnicity to tolerance for risk to approaches to problem solving. As you learn about the range of possible ways of being, you can better understand those around you as well as yourself.

When, for example, you hear how differently someone else approaches a situation or how she feels about risk-taking, you learn about that person and that type of style as well as how to better understand your own preferences. You learn to see your way and that of others more relatively and can accept a larger range of options for how people approach things.

Because personal styles and cultural backgrounds can vary greatly among people, these differences can become sources of frustration. At the same time, such differences offer the nutrients of creativity and innovation. When you learn to see differences as complementary, contributing something that's been missing, you can use them as strengths for the group rather than as frustrations.

I like to take a group through a series of exercises to help members see the diversity of styles that are present. The outcome is usually great laughter and sighs of relief as people experience deep recognition of themselves and their coworkers, along with renewed appreciation for each other. Then we can approach ways to work with those differences.

Multicultural or diversity training can help people understand differing experiences arising from ethnicity and race. The opportunity is to learn to listen culturally: to hear and understand people as individuals and to lose the stereotypes of cultures that typecast people. When these programs create open conversations in a safe environment where everyone can be authentic, this experience transfers to everyday situations and promotes a more creative workplace.

Such programs also need to open awareness about the structural ways in which racism and power relationships between different social groups shape our experiences and therefore, our assumptions, our expectations, what we imagine possible, and how others view and treat us. Entrenched prejudices mean that it can be difficult for anyone different to appear credible. Difference in culture can mean differences in participation and opportunities. Building awareness in this area offers opportunities to remove structural limitations to people's full engagement.

Mastery in Group Culture and Process: Powerful groups attend to the interpersonal nature of their work. This means they realize there are dynamics in groups that require

Areas for Development	Personal Effectiveness	Multicultural Competence	Group Effectiveness

• Personality
• Culture/ethnicity/race
• Values/comfort zones
• Learning styles
• Decision styles
• Handling conflict
• Emotional intelligence
• Leadership style
• Communication
    Managing inferences and assumptions
    Listening
    Negotiating
• Mind-set/mental frameworks
	• Learning to understand and work with your personal styles and strengths	• Learning to understand and work with the strengths and styles of other people	• Integrating differences and working with the dynamics of groups

Special Skills	**Personal Performance** • Job expertise • Stress prevention and management • Optimizing capabilities	**Valuing Diversity** • Interest • Acceptance • Valuing • Understanding and eliminating structural and institutional discrimination	**Group Skills** • Shared leadership • Knowledge of group dynamics • Group culture • Facilitation skills

special understanding and attention. They learn about the habits and strategies that bring diverse contributions together in a coherent fashion, turning the distinctiveness of each person in the group into collective accomplishment.

Attention to group dynamics means looking at what happens when multiple people interact routinely: this may be in a work group, an organization, or a society. Different disciplines approach this from their own lenses, all of which offer important insights into what will help groups perform better.

Psychologists examine the tensions between individual needs and group needs and how those tensions can play out in psychological struggles. Social psychologists look at how groups develop a distinct identity and generate their own psychological dynamics apart from the individuals in them.

Anthropologists observe how a group develops an identity and culture, distinct from any individual in it, as people "go along to get along." We look at how norms, shared beliefs, and ideas form the ways individuals view the world. At the heart of this approach is the understanding that people attach meaning to a group's behaviors, interactions, experiences, and creations; this meaning in turn makes up the culture that shapes their behavior.

In addition to learning to recognize and work productively with group dynamics and culture, it is important to learn effective process skills for meetings, collaborative decision making, and group problem solving.

Group Alchemy gives even veteran managers the working tools essential to improve personal relationships, at work and at home.

Group Alchemy is an essential tool for all managers who value their impact on organizational and personal performance. It gives even veteran managers the working tools essential to improve personal relationships, at work and at home. This excellent book provides step-by-step techniques to improve morale—and results—for everyone.

—Ken Graham, former CEO, El Camino Hospital, Mountain View, California, recipient of the American College of Health Care Executives 2011 Gold Medal for local, regional and national service.

Deborah Pruitt offers a new way of thinking about groups and redefines the nature of the work experience ... powered by energy, optimism, and inspiration.

We live in a brave new world of global change. What hasn't changed for many is a work experience centered on survival where people feel they have to armor themselves for safety. Into this environment *Group Alchemy* brings daylight, clarity, and a different picture of the management universe, one filled with alternative possibilities. Writing in a supportive, conversational tone, Deborah Pruitt offers a new way of thinking about groups and redefines the nature of the work experience and how to create a group culture of success. Is it possible to be true to yourself while working with a team in which all members actively participate? This book says, "Yes!" The practical tools it presents here for doing just that are powered by energy, optimism, and inspiration. I'm glad to have discovered *Group Alchemy!*

—Roger S. Mason, Health, Education, and Training Consultant

It shows that groups can be positively influenced by even the slightest change in a single group member.

This book speaks to the alchemical nature of group change and offers an effective system to achieve it. It shows that groups can be positively influenced by even the slightest change in a single group member; before reading *Group Alchemy*, I hadn't realized that each individual has so much power.

— BB Borowitz, founder, Dance Your One Wondrous Life

Group Alchemy is an inspiring call to action for all of us to participate actively and wisely in the organizations through which we live our lives.

Deborah Pruitt's book on organizational dynamics and transformation is distinctive and significant for a number of reasons. First, she brings the perspective of an academic anthropologist who knows and appreciates the role of culture in the domain of collective activity. Like a good anthropologist and unlike most organizational consultants, she tells stories and offers concrete examples to inform us, motivate us, and stimulate our thinking. In fact, she reminds us of the power stories have to create our cultures and our lives. She also brings her extensive practical experience as an organizational consultant. The result is a book that is both clear and complex—one that provides a coherent theoretical framework, clear principles, tangible techniques and tips, and thought-provoking questions, while not overlooking the invariable subtleties and complexities that are essential to our understanding of our lives in organizations. The book contains a depth of sophistication and wisdom not usually found in a simple self-help manual, yet we are also given practical suggestions and food for thought usually not found in an academic or theoretical analysis of organizations.

Most of all, *Group Alchemy* is an inspiring call to action for all of us to participate actively and wisely in the organizations through which we live our lives. Dr. Pruitt invites us to engage with her in learning how to create transformative cultures within these organizations, and to do so in active and constructive cooperation with others.

—John Bilorusky, founder and director, Western Institute for Social Research

About the Author

When Deborah Pruitt left corporate America to study successful alternatives to traditional bureaucratic organizations, she found that the reasons for their success were clearly rooted in their cultures. With a fellowship from the National Science Foundation, she studied grassroots organizations in island nations such as Jamaica, Fiji, the Cook Islands, and Vanuatu. Further observations in Australia, Tanzania, Europe, and Scandinavia deepened her understanding of longstanding cultural dynamics and how all groups can benefit from engaging them with intention and purpose. Deborah earned a PhD in anthropology from the University of California at Berkeley. She now serves on the faculty at the Western Institute for Social Research in Berkeley and is president of Group Alchemy Consulting.

From civic organizations like the City of Piedmont to nonprofits like Survivor's International and Community Resources for Science to institutions like Kaiser Medical Center and the University of California, for more than twenty years Deborah Pruitt has taught groups how to do their best work together, no matter what they're up against. An author and public speaker on the subject of group alchemy, she offers workshops, programs, and coaching in cultural strategies for powerful collaboration. www.groupalchemy.net.

CPSIA information can be obtained at www.ICGtesting.com
Printed in the USA
BVOW03s1601200114

342328BV00006B/10/P